...not just an ordinary pony

m.e. colman

BookBaby
7905 N Crescent Blvd
Pennsauken, NJ 08110
https://www.bookbaby.com/
1-877-961-6878

To order more copies:
https://store.bookbaby.com/book/not-just-an-ordinary-pony

Book Design and all graphics   M.E. Colman
Cover Design and back   M.E. Colman

"…not just an ordinary pony"
by M.E. Colman
A CSJB Book

ISBN: 978-1-09839-892-7

Dear Joy,

I have spent many retreat hours at this wonderful Episcopal Convent in Mendham, NJ. I don't remember the Pony — but remember the nuns, dogs, and cats! I love how this story developed from a collection of stories — and I know how

a CSJB book

much you love horses and writing!

Merry Christmas!

2021

All my love and faith,
Oma Beth

Community St. John Baptist
Mendham, New Jersey

In gratitude to the Community of St John Baptist

Chapters

"…if only he could talk."

Have any of you ever attempted to write a book? Well, it is rather daunting, to say the least. Remember when we were learning to drive? Or ride a bike? All the stops and starts along the way… yet we all persevered, didn't we?

Most of you who are reading this know us well, and for years so many have asked if we might write a book about our beloved pony. And for those of you who aren't quite familiar with us or our life, this is a true story of a small horse, a pony. He was not just an ordinary pony, but a beautiful, magical, mystical creature who appeared on our grounds many years ago…

Writing the book was not unlike putting together the pieces of a jig-saw puzzle, or connecting the dots that form an amazing picture. You will see how so many of the missing pieces of that jigsaw puzzle fall into place when you read the stories shared by individuals who had significant parts to play in those early days and weeks after the pony arrived.

The first half of the book will be a narrative part, with sketches, a few newspaper articles, numerous color illustrations in a watercolor style, and countless anecdotal stories. And for the cat and dog lovers, we thought you might like to meet our other four-legged friends who lived with us during all those years the pony was here. Brief profiles of that cast of characters will also be included.

Throughout the time our boy was with us we had a newsletter that came out three times throughout the year. Often people told us how much they enjoyed the articles "written" by our furry four-legged residents. Hence with that in mind, the second half of the book will be reprints of the pony's column "Pony's Point of View" with the accompanying black and white photographs.

When the pony came into our lives, we think he was around 7 or 8 years old. A few of us thought he might have originally been from out West, shipped to the East Coast with other wild horses in boxcars on a train. It sounds rather farfetched, but who knows? Although we knew nothing about his past or his "childhood," we can only imagine…

This little guy touched so many people's lives over the years. It's only fitting to tell his story.

So, the only place to begin is at the very beginning…

It was early April, a gorgeous spring afternoon, yet somewhat chilly. The leaves on the trees were just budding out, that fresh yellow green against an iridescent blue sky. Several of us thought we'd go for a walk to see if the daffodils were up yet, over by the pond. We knew exactly where to find them, as that's where they are every year.

We started down our drive, turning just before the litchgate to the cemetery. Leaving the expanse of lawn behind us, we entered the woods and followed the worn path we knew so well, pausing to see some snowdrops just making their way up through the dried oak leaves, their heads still drooped from all that pushing through the earth (it takes a lot of effort to come to life.)

Quietly we continued along the path, not speaking a word to one another. Our pace quickened as we neared the clearing where we hoped to find the daffodils. Indeed, we were not disappointed… there they were in their glorious yellow splendor, yet appearing a little ragged around the edges from their struggle to be born.

Deciding to wait until more daffodils appeared in the days to come before we picked any, we continued along our way.

Walking past the pond, we then headed toward the old hockey field, behind the school.

And that's when we saw him.

We stopped short in our tracks, not quite believing our eyes. At first glance we thought it was a cow, as the coloring was similar to a Guernsey. It was far enough away so we weren't sure. But wait a minute, there aren't any dairy farms nearby. How could a cow be loose on our property?

The creature must have been startled, because he raised his head from grazing, and immediately trotted off into the woods nearby. We then could see that it was clearly not a cow, but a beautiful horse.

As we excitedly made our way back to the house, our minds were racing. Where did he come from? Who did he belong to? We were aware that there was a farm across Route 24 where they boarded horses. Perhaps it ran away. We looked up the phone number for Backer Farm and called them to inquire if they were missing a horse. No, they weren't.

The following afternoon a few of us went out to the same location where we saw him the previous day, but to no avail (now with some afterthought, it would be highly unlikely if we found him in that exact place where he was the day before.) So, we figured he might have made his way home, wherever that was... or his owner came for him.

3

It was getting late, and we didn't want to miss Vespers. Fully aware that it's not every day a small horse appears on your property, we knew we'd be coming over often to look for our surprise visitor, our unexpected mystery guest.

So, we headed back, walking again into the coolness of the woods. And there he stood, behind a tree, watching us, and appearing rather groggy. As he was only about 20 feet away, we could get a better look at him. He was a lot smaller than how he appeared when we first saw him the previous day, and somewhat shaggy and dirty. He was wearing a halter that was much too big for him, and overall had the appearance of a lost soul.

The days that followed morphed one into the other. A few of us would still go out to look for the pony, often seeing him grazing over behind the school, or near the pond. We couldn't understand why no one was searching for him (we had no idea there were others out there trying to catch him.)

At some point in the weeks that followed, one of our sisters was down at the Post Office in town, and a Police officer who happened to be in there at the same time recognized her. He asked if that horse was still up on our property. He said the pony was causing a lot of trouble wandering back and forth across Route 24. They were concerned the pony would be hit by a car. He was also seen alongside the road licking the salt left from a few late winter snowstorms. The officer told her the chief of police gave them orders to shoot if they saw him.

Well, that's all we had to hear to start taking the reins in our own hands (sorry, no pun intended.) To be honest, I didn't have a clue as to how to properly care for a horse. But one learns very quickly in certain extenuating circumstances.

We called Mr. Backer again, the man who owned the place that boarded the horses. He suggested putting out a salt lick near the pond, as well as giving the pony some sweet feed to supplement the grass he was getting (as a side note, sweet feed is a mixture of oats and molasses.) And they made their own special blend over at the farm, which would be very convenient to say the least.

Out we went to a feed and grain store in Bernardsville to buy a small black rubber tub for his oats, and a salt block. After returning, we then carried them over to the pond, placing them both in the grass. Every day, rain or shine, I would take his delicious molasses oats out to the same spot in an empty cottage cheese container, pouring the contents into the rubber tub.

As time went on, it seemed to fall to me by default to shoulder the full responsibility of this special creature. At first it was quite the novelty for all of us to have a little horse on our property, but it was becoming very apparent that this might be for the long haul. He needed attention, care, and commitment, so yours truly stepped up to the plate, so to speak. To be perfectly honest, I always wanted a horse, and dreamed of having one from the time I was about 10 years old.

One day when walking over from St. Marguerites our retreat house, to my surprise two figures on two large dappled white horses were coming up our old back road, heading across our grounds. Calling out, "may I help you?" seemed the appropriate thing to say rather than, "hello, this is private property." After all, it's not every day when you see two riders on horseback on your front lawn, much less the grounds of a convent.

The two were an interesting pair. One was a woman, blondish, appearing rather small to be riding such a large horse. And the other person was seemingly a tall man, sitting very straight in the saddle, with a lasso hanging over his shoulder. Hm, I wondered, are they the owners coming to rope the pony…

A soft-spoken female voice responded from atop the one horse saying she was the owner (ah ha!) and asked if it was all right to be there. She seemed apologetic in her tone. My immediate response was, "of course," but really wasn't all that sure I wanted them to catch him!

As they rode down our road a thought ran through my mind to call out to them, saying, "good luck." But I refrained. After all, that little guy was already becoming a part of our lives.

But in a more reflective moment, I had to admit, if it were meant to be, let it be so... (just as an aside, he was still there when we went out later in the day to see if they'd caught him. Oh, thank God.)

It might be mentioned that the small woman on the horse was Rebecca Backer, but please remember we learned this only in retrospect. She shares her side of the story later in the book. If Rebecca hadn't followed her heart and bought the pony at an auction, our little guy would never have been a part of our lives. It all started at that auction…

In the weeks that followed, we could only piece together the events that occurred in those early days. At first, we were totally oblivious to the comings and goings and all the activity happening right on our property, over in the woods and by the pond where our boy could be found grazing.

So, here is what we learned:

Some people who lived near Backer Farm bought a pony for their kids at an auction. The new owners couldn't get near him the following day to clean his stall. They let him out into the larger area of the barn, but someone opened the barn door, of course unaware of the situation. The pony then bolted, seizing the opportunity to claim his freedom. They immediately tried to catch him, but could not get near him. He began wandering back and forth across Route 24, and was seen along the road by motorists. That's when we learned the police were given instructions to shoot on sight...

The pony was hanging out more and more behind the old school building, near the pond and in the nearby woods. The owners persevered in trying their best to catch him, but to no avail. Rodeo ropers and mounted police were called in. A local vet tried shooting him with tranquilizer darts numerous times. Nothing seemed to work. The pony evaded them, running into the wooded area where they couldn't get to him.

Days, then weeks passed, and the little guy was still there. I continued to walk out to the pond with the cottage cheese container of sweet feed. It was becoming a daily ritual. The pony began appearing around that same time of day. Always maintaining a safe distance from me, he'd continue his grazing, watching me from the corner of his eye.

One afternoon I'd headed out to the pond, and the pony was grazing in front of Mr. Craigy's cottage at the time.

Just after finishing pouring the sweet oats into his bowl, there was this ungodly squawking coming from the woods nearby. Suddenly a wild turkey appeared, running directly toward me. I was motionless, not quite sure what to do. The pony moved quickly forward, and then stood directly between me and the big bird, clearly blocking the forward momentum of the turkey. The feathered creature was undoubtedly surprised, promptly running off, and disappearing behind the underbrush.

It took a moment or two to catch my breath, at which point only then did it occur to me what the pony had actually done...

On another occasion, as I was walking along the well-worn path through the woods with his sweet feed, Mr.

8

Pony met me halfway. He knew exactly what was in my hand. He didn't budge. So, sitting down on a fallen tree I thought maybe he'd come over and might eat from the container. Ever so slowly, so tentatively, he inched his way toward those wonderful molasses oats! Holding the container just under his nose, after getting a whiff of what was there, he put his nose into it (not without making a mess.) Some of the oats went flying to the ground, but most were still left in the container. The second time he attempted it he was a little more careful, and could see I wasn't about to try to put a rope around his neck or try to catch him. It was definitely a breakthrough, a turning point in building trust.

From then on it became a game. I'd never know where the pony would show up. If he wasn't out in his usual habitat behind the school near the pond, he would appear along the path in the woods. If the sweet feed was still in my hands, we'd do our little routine of him sometimes eating from the container, sometimes not… it always depended on what kind of mood that guy was in. And this is something we learned as time went on, that the pony was totally unpredictable. Right up until his very last breath, we could never guess how he was going to respond.

Spring merged into summer, then early fall. By then we began to see our boy grazing on the lawn near the cemetery. He had ventured from the pond, following the path through the woods. On one such afternoon, sweet feed in hand, I happened to see him down there. I walked past him, sat on the steps of the litchgate, and waited…

Gradually he worked his way over toward me, quite nonchalantly of course. I learned if I shook the container, he would recognize the sound of the oats and it helped to encourage him to come closer. The patience it took was not always easy, but it was all part of getting him to trust more.

When he put his nose into the container, I sometimes raised it slightly so he would get used to a little pressure, keeping in mind that someday we'd be able to touch him.

That's right. All these weeks and he would not allow us to touch him. Occasionally he would gently nudge my arm or shoulder with his nose, but when I reached my hand toward him, he would turn his head or back away.

What was his story? Had he been abused? If only he could talk... so many questions. Where did he come from? He didn't have any calloused areas around the corners of his mouth to indicate that he'd worn a bit and bridle. We heard that sometimes wild horses are rounded up out West and brought East on trains, transported in boxcars to sell at auctions. You don't want to know where many of them end up. But the pony caught the attention of that person who bid for him. She fell in love with this beautiful little horse.

***

Months had already passed, and having felt responsible for this very special guy day after day, it occurred to me that the pony could not continue living out there the way he had in the spring and summer. Warm weather is one thing, but braving the elements of winter was a different story.

And with the fall approaching, a very serious concern was just beginning to surface. Hunting season would be starting in late autumn. The woods behind the school were often frequented by uninvited hunters. And often they hunt illegally at night, shooting at anything that moves. The pony's life would be in danger.

As the days grew shorter and the nights colder, we sometimes heard our guy on the front cloister, his hooves making quite the racket. Admittedly the grass out front is always green and succulent, but we also realized he was lingering closer to the house.

A thought began to cross my mind, and wouldn't go away. What if we built a shed for him, and set up fencing in the back, why couldn't we give him the protection he needed?

Now, we live in a monastic setting, following a Rule of life. No one of us can just decide to bring home a cat or a dog, certainly not a small horse, without receiving the permission from the rest of the community. Quite frankly, it was rather daunting for me to even think of it, to have to say something to the entire group. I was just a novice at the time, new to the religious life.

Most of the sisters (only 7 life-professed then) would probably not speak up. But it would be the Mother Superior Emeritus, Margaret Helena, that might say something. If I may, let me add that she was a formidable figure, if not even a bit scary, to me anyway. Ah, but I knew she grew up on a ranch on the plains of South Dakota. And she had her own horse. So, with that in mind, I finally mustered up enough courage and presented my request.

As expected, no one spoke at first, but after what seemed like an endless silence, Sr. Margaret Helena said, slowly and deliberately, "if you can find the money for fencing and a shed, as well as take responsibility for his care, I don't see why he couldn't stay."

With that endorsement and seal of approval, the wheels of change were set in motion! Never could we possibly know what the future would bring, and how this little horse would change all our lives...

Sister Margaret Helena chatting with the pony

"…a free spirit that transcended the ordinary."

After getting the green light to go forward, we wanted to reach as many people as possible, so we got in touch with the Observer Tribune, a small local newspaper (these were the days before the internet.) The article was entitled *"Stray pony, 'adopted' by nuns, prompts 'Save the Pony' campaign."* It went into some detail about him being loose on our property for months, and along with hunting season and winter looming up in the near future, fencing and a shed had to be built so he would be protected.

To our surprise, the response to the article was beyond our hopes and expectations. Checks started coming in from our friends, associates of the community and family members, as well as from strangers. Some were quite generous ($250, $500.) One favorite donation from a local Brownie troop arrived in bills and loose coins, about $37 and some change in total. We were just so touched by the overall response. And so very grateful.

Oh, before continuing with the pony story, let's tell you how we came up with giving our sweet boy a name. In the Old Testament, the act of naming someone or something implied the "namer" exercising a kind of power over the named, as shown in the naming of the animals in Genesis. God gave the human the right to name all animals and, at the same time, dominion over them.

We realized early on that we really had no power or control over our boy, and he certainly lived up to that. As the years went by, he never disappointed us to be sure. You will see as the story unravels how incorrigible he truly was, right up to his last breath. This little guy was much more than what he appeared to be. He was the embodiment of the essence of a small horse, with a free spirit that transcended the ordinary…

Let's get back to the Observer Tribune. The original article was much too small, so it is printed in a larger format so you can read it.

Observer~Tribune

Thursday, September 24, 1992
by Cheryl L. Kornfield, Staff Writer

Stray pony, 'adopted' by nuns, prompts 'Save the Pony' campaign

MENDHAM - Ownerless, homeless and nameless are a few words to describe a pony seen roaming around the Saint John Baptist Convent grounds off route 24.

With hunting season opening this weekend, some fear the pony could get killed in the wooded area surrounding the convent.

Sister Margo Elizabeth of the convent, who has been caring for the pony along with other sisters, wants to give the stray pony a home, and figures there couldn't be a more perfect place than a fenced off tract of their 60 to 70 acres of land.

The sisters' only problem is a lack of funds to build a fence and a shed for the brown and white colored Indian pony.

"We have to fence him in and build a shed," Sister Elizabeth said. "We have to protect him; it's giving him sanctuary."

To give the pony his freedom, rather than allowing him to be captured and taken away, the sisters decided they would try to raise the money to build a fence. Sister Elizabeth said the sisters are planning to purchase a basic fence for about $1500 which would extend to about one acre of their property, just enough land for the pony.

Some area residents have already contributed to the "pony fund" which began last week.

14

The equine, which the sisters simply call "Pony," was temporarily owned by a local resident who purchased the animal at an auction. The owner kept him until he ran away.

Since April, the pony has roamed the property of Saint John Baptist. He was discovered by the sisters, who contacted the owner who, in turn, told them he decided he didn't want to keep him since he was wild, Sister Elizabeth said.

Since the former owner has small children, he realized it may be dangerous to care for the animal. As a result, the former owner donated the pony to the convent and plans to help raise the funds to build a fence.

Although the pony may be wild, Sister Elizabeth said he has not been mean to anyone so far at the convent. "Everyone who sees him falls in love with him," she said. "He's shown no signs of being mean; if anything, he's been a clown."

Sister Elizabeth said the pony is frightened, and she thinks it may have been mistreated. There were a number of unsuccessful attempts to capture him in April. "We can't really touch him," she said, adding that the sisters are able to feed him oats and molasses out of a bucket.

Getting the fence built soon is important, she said, since hunting season begins this weekend. The convent's property borders other wooded properties that permit hunting.

"If the pony is running free in the woods his life is endangered," Elizabeth said. "We want to give him a protected home."

Anyone interested in helping to protect the pony can send donations to "Save the Pony Fund" at St. John Baptist, Box 240, Mendham, NJ 07945

Shortly after the Observer Tribune printed their little story, a larger local newspaper, the Morristown Daily Record, wanted to run their own article, along with a color photo.

15

The pony was becoming a celebrity! The article, written by Christine Federico, appeared on the front page of the weekend section. Chris Pedota took the photograph that caught so many people's attention. Roberta Shields, a local woman who saw the article, was so moved with the photograph that she did a painting of the photo and wanted to give it to us. Roberta has since become a dear friend of the community, and tells her story later in the book.

Here's a larger reprint of the article:

Daily Record (Morristown, New Jersey) · 23 Oct 1992, Fri · Page 1

Wild Pony Reined in at Convent

"Sister Margo Elizabeth feeds a pony that has found happiness, and a home, at St. John the Baptist Convent in Mendham Township. After running away from owners, a veterinarian and a rodeo roper, it seems the nuns have a calming effect on the feisty critter who is nicknamed 'the Devil Pony.' 'He has been able to avoid the glue factory. He has been able to remain free.' Sister Margo said. 'We just want him to remain free, and if he allows us to pet him or brush him, fine.'"

(continued on p. 4)

'Devil Pony' finds a home with nuns

Hyper horse eludes all others

By CHRISTINE FEDERICO
Daily Record

MENDHAM TWP. — "A runaway pony that has escaped its owners, police, a professional rodeo roper and a veterinarian who shot it five times with tranquilizers has found sanctuary with the only humans it trusts — a convent of nuns.

The brown and white pinto was nicknamed 'The Devil Pony' by borough and township police because for weeks they chased him through yards and over state highways - to no avail. Now he seems to have settled on two acres at the St. John the Baptist convent where he happily munches the fruit off apple trees, said the nuns, who call him 'Pony.'

The nuns are using snow fencing to keep Pony from wandering into wooded areas where hunting season is in full swing. They have raised about $1,200 of an estimated $2,000 they need to buy a post-and-rail fence and a shed so he will be warm during the winter.

'He seems happy,' said Sister Margo Elizabeth, one of eight Episcopal nuns who live there. 'He's almost oblivious to the fencing. You never see him go up to it and stop short and act upset. He seems pretty content.'

Pony came to the Mendhams after being saved from the dog meat factory in April, when an animal-loving Mendham Borough family paid $200 for him at an auction. He appeared docile but when he entered his new stall he turned his hind legs toward the entrance and seemed ready to kick. Any quick movement from his owners made him run to the other side of the stall.

He couldn't be touched.

17

After three days, Pony ran out the barn's open door, stopping to graze on the front lawn. The family took off after him, and the chase was on.

'I had him for three days, and I didn't even get to touch him,' said the owner, who wouldn't give her name.

For the next two weeks, just about everything was done to round up the hyper little horse. Police chased him with poles that have loops on the end; the county's mounted park police were called in with the hope that their horses would calm him.

A Bernardsville veterinarian shot five tranquilizers into his side - enough for a 2,000-pound horse, the owner said. But the tranquilizers only seemed to spur Pony on.

'We were running through the whole woods to try to get him,' the owner said. 'He was just too smart.'

By then Pony was leaving his calling card on the lawns of some very expensive homes, and residents were calling police daily with Pony sightings.

Exasperated, the owner called a professional lasso man from Pennsylvania, whose sole accomplishment was to chase Pony across Route 24 and into the 60 acres of land where the nuns live.

The skittish Pony had the run of the convent all summer, and came to trust the nuns, especially Sister Margo, who would feed him oats.

At first he would approach the oats only if she wasn't nearby. Now, after looking to make sure no one else is around, Pony will cautiously eat the oats while Sister Margo holds the bucket. Any loud voices or sharp movements still frighten him.

'The pony has added a dimension to our lives, too,' Sister Margo said. 'When we go downtown, people will ask us about the pony. Everybody knows about the pony. It's almost like having a child in the family. Everybody asks how he is doing.'

She said Pony helps to provide an uplift to people on religious retreats at the convent."

18

Before long we raised enough for the fencing. We had to decide where we wanted the circumscribed area, and which type of fencing would be the easiest to put up, and the least expensive. We were fortunate to have part of the proposed area for the parameter already in place - the convent building and the apple orchard at one end, as well as the long monastic wall running along the length of our former Victorian English garden.

The inherent contour of the remaining property provided a natural boundary, so we put up the snow fencing where the wooded area met the lawn. Aesthetically speaking, snow fencing was not the preferred choice or option. But it worked, and the price was right. We did use some post and rail fence up nearer the back of the house and the garages where it was more visible.

Once the fencing was done, we then needed shelter for our boy. After doing some "research" we found Brady Sheds, a place in New Jersey that made pool cabanas and sheds. We chose the perfect design that originally had a small window with shutters, and even a window box for flowers! So the location for Pony's little house was determined, and a date set for when they'd come with the materials.

About a week later, a truck arrived in the morning and the shed was finished before it got dark. We couldn't believe it was completed in one day.

During his lunch break, one of the guys was listening to his radio. He heard on WNEW news about a "wild pony" that ended up on the property of a convent in Mendham, New Jersey. At first he thought he was just building a tool shed, but then began to wonder when we requested flooring that would withstand some weight. After asking a few questions, the young man only then realized that he was at that convent mentioned on WNEW. He wanted so much to see the pony, but we said he was still way back in the woods.

We now had a little house and fencing for our boy. Obviously, the one missing ingredient was the little guy himself! As mentioned earlier, he was grazing closer and closer to the convent building, often seen out front.

The dilemma that arose was how could we get him to the back and into his new enclosure? He was not going to allow us to just walk up to him and put a rope around his neck (like any normal horse) and lead him to the back. We had to come up with another idea…

As you already know, Pony loved his molasses oats… we would just wait until we saw him out front, and with container in hand, get close enough to him so he'd get a whiff of his beloved sweet feed. We would then try to encourage him to follow, leading him around back. In order to begin to implement our proposed grand scheme, there was some preparation to be done. Two rails in the post and rail fence needed to be removed, and his familiar black rubber tub had to be placed inside the enclosure. So, we had a plan.

One fine day in September someone reported seeing the pony grazing on our lawn in front of the convent.

It was time for action…

Moving quickly, we put the grain in the cottage cheese container, and checked to be sure his "bowl" was in place inside the enclosed area. We then removed the two fence rails. All was ready.

Oh, so very casually, I walked around to the front with his delicious sweet feed and approached our boy. It had to be done very carefully. If not, he would just trot off into the sunset… Closer and closer, taking little steps, I inched nearer to the pony until he got the scent of the molasses. He proceeded to chew on a clump of grass, eyeing the container, clearly thinking… should he interrupt his grazing and walk over toward me, or continue what he was doing. One thing we learned about this guy over the years was that he responded in his own time, whenever he was ready.

It felt like an eternity, standing there waiting for this character, but he eventually moved toward me and the molasses oats. Okay I thought, the first stage, the preparatory one, was done. Now was the hard part. The container had to be just under his nose, moving it slightly as to not allow him from getting into the grain. Ever so slowly, together we headed in the direction of the driveway and the garages, I walking backwards, with Pony's nose only inches from the container.

When we did reach the asphalt, the sound of his hooves on the hard surface appeared to startle him because he hesitated. But then we continued our way towards the fencing, s l o w l y. He seemed to become aware of the different setting, moving his head from side to side, noticing the carport on the left, garages on the right. Occasionally he'd pause, but as soon as that container was brought up just under his nose, it was enough to distract him from the strange surroundings.

21

Oh, those cars that were parked there! He seemed to take everything in...

It seemed endless, but we finally reached the post and rail fence. Yet again, he stopped. Oh no, please, Pony, we've come this far! I walked inside the enclosure and rather loudly poured the oats into his bowl, being sure he heard the container hitting the bottom.

Then he took one step, and another, gradually making his way between the two posts. Then turning toward his bowl, he reached his oats, and happily began munching on his meal.

Very tentatively, moving as unobtrusively as possible, I put the two rails back into place, and breathed a long, deep sigh of relief.
He was home at last...

In the days that followed, the pony didn't seem to be aware that he was fenced in. After all, he was already familiar with the apple orchard and the area behind the convent. It was a large enough space, so we hoped he'd still feel free and not enclosed. He seemed to be happy enough back there grazing to his heart's content.

We were sure to continue with the same late afternoon schedule for his molasses oats, and added a morning feeding.

Ah, but this was only the beginning! There is a lot to learn when fostering a beautiful small horse for the first time. Each day was a new experience. We were very lucky to have Mr. Backer and the farm so nearby. With the boarding of the horses, they always had some hay available for the pony. And they made their own molasses oats, so it was always available. Driving the truck down there to the barn to pick up the hay and the sweet feed became a highlight in the week for me. Fred (Mr. Backer) always greeted me with a warm smile. It never occurred to me how strange it might have looked for a nun in full habit to be pulling up to the barn in a truck...

We continued to put out a trace mineral salt block, and were diligent in providing fresh water. Of course, our boy needed "bedding" in his shed! During the early years Pony was with us, we were able to find everything we needed at the feed and grain store in Bernardsville (where we got his salt lick and black rubber "cereal bowl.") He eventually grew to love the scent of the pine shavings, but not in the beginning...

One guarantee we have here on the East coast is the unerring fact that seasons change. And indeed they do... The very first year the pony was with us we had a blizzard in March, '93.

It might be pointed out that Pony did not go into his shed at first (very much "an outdoorsman.") We were very worried he'd get a chill or even worse. Yet he always seemed to find shelter of some sort or another. There were times when we couldn't find him at first because he wasn't anywhere up in the front near his shed. Eventually we found him going under the summer houses where it was protected from the elements.

As it was way back in his large enclosure, too far to be able to keep an eye on him, we decided to close off the upper smaller enclosure at night so he'd be nearer to us and the house.

In order to encourage the pony to spend more time in his shed, we literally cut out the end wall, the one with a southerly exposure. We then raised it to be an overhang, held up with posts. Our nature boy could stand under the overhang, not only protected from the snow and freezing rain, but also the north wind. And because that whole end of the structure was open, he then started to spend more time inside the shed itself. Thank God.

***

That following spring was one we would never forget. We knew the pony needed his shots and should be checked out by a vet. We called Fred Backer again (God bless him) and he recommended the animal hospital they used for their horses. But there was that persistent issue of not being able to approach the pony or get near him. How could they examine him, much less administer an injection? How could they administer his vaccines if he wouldn't let anyone near him? He'd have to be sedated. Again, we needed a plan...

We first tried putting something in his feed to sedate him. But that didn't work. The vet then suggested catching him and tranquilizing him with an injection. That sounds easy enough, doesn't it? If you recall our "wild guy" had a history of not getting caught.

So not without a lot of maneuvering, one lovely spring day Fred Backer came over with several others, including one of his sons and a grandson. The vet then arrived along with a farrier - who had been a former rodeo roper.

The event began. It took several hours to catch the pony before they eventually roped him. Once the tranquilizer was administered by injection, he finally succumbed to the sedation. The team had to work quickly before it wore off. His feet were trimmed, he had a thorough physical exam, and he received all his vaccines.

"...this beautiful untouchable pony."

In the next few chapters, we'd like to write about the memories and anecdotal stories shared by several of the people already mentioned.

Rebecca was the woman who first bid on the pony at an auction in the spring of 1992. She seemed pleased to be able to tell her story.

"Hello Sister Margo,
Here is my account of how I acquired the pony.
When we moved to Mendham, we had a 5 stall barn. I had my first daughter, who was 2 at the time. My Mom and Dad were living with us at the time. All of us were novices to the horse ownership game. I decided that I wanted to get my daughter a pony. My Dad and I heard of a livestock auction in South Jersey called Budgies (I believe that was the name). My Mom, Dad and I thought we would take a day trip down to see what the auction was like, not thinking we would come home with a pony.

Well, there before us was the sweetest, most gorgeous pony I have ever seen. I just had to have him. We didn't have any way to bring a pony home but my dad bid on him anyway. I was so excited to win the auction, I can't remember how much we paid for him. We asked the owner of the pony if he knew anyone who would bring the pony to our barn, he happily agreed to bring him. I had not touched the pony at this point but he looked so sweet and gentle.

I was so happy with the way the day went and couldn't wait to get my new pony home to show my daughter. We arrived home and the man unloaded the pony leading him right into the stall and then promptly left. That's when the trouble started. The first hour I was able to pet our new boy, since it was late, I left the barn for some sleep and would see him in the morning....

I rushed out to see him in the morning and it was like a new pony was slipped in during the night. I couldn't touch him. I couldn't even enter the stall. I didn't know what to do. I called the farmer up the road because he ran a boarding facility so I figured he would have some ideas. He said the pony was probably drugged and now it was worn off. He told me to leave him alone to let him get settled and to try to hold an apple by the door to get him to come near. I tried apples, carrots, sugar cubes, nothing was getting him to come close. I would just open the door to throw hay in and pour the feed through the stall bars.

We were having family over that weekend so of course I wanted everyone to see this beautiful untouchable pony. After taking everyone out to the barn, family hung behind trying to get the pony to take the apple. Someone (no one copped to being the last one out, it's still mystery) didn't close the barn door tight enough. Well within an hour I saw my beautiful pony run out the driveway.

I didn't have a clue what to do... I called the farmer up the road again, Fred Backer, who became my father-in-law, to see if he could help me catch him. His son Steve, who became my husband, was away in Florida, but he said he would come and help. We tried to find him, all day. Neighbors were also trying to help. When it was getting dark and late we decided to call it a night and start again in the morning. I called the police to let them know what was going on.

My adorable pony had become a nightmare. I renamed him my "Devil Pony." He seemed to hang around a home between Roxciticus Rd. and Rt. 24. So, I had a vet come out and try to tranquilize him. (I can't remember what vet, sorry. Might have been someone I got the name from the mounted police.) First we tried putting the sedation in his food but couldn't tell if he or something else was eating it

27

because it was having no effect. The vet came out again and tried to use a blow gun to get the tranquilizer dart into him. He was a great shot. The "Devil" pony was running around and his adrenaline was so high that it cancelled out the meds so the vet shot him again. He still didn't go down. The Mounted police come out to try to catch him. They were great riders but didn't have the skill to rope him. The vet suggested I call a roper from PA. I got the gentleman to come out and after hours of running around he couldn't catch him either because the pony would run into the thicket.

I really didn't know what I was going to do. By the end of the week the police said they would have to shoot him if I didn't catch him because he has been going down to Rt. 24 at night and licking the salt off the road and would eventually cause an accident. That's when I heard he was hanging around up with you. His Savior.

My husband, Steve Backer, told me you were going to build a fence around him because he was hanging out around your kitchen. I remember going up to you and discussing a plan of attack. My memory is a little sketchy on what happened next. Steve reminded me about the vet visit to give him his shots and to check him over once he was fenced in at your place. He recounts that the vet tranquilized him, and Steve knelt down on the pony's neck because since he seemed unaffected by the tranquilizers, the vet didn't want him to come out of it by surprise. The pony in fact did come out of it and bit my husband's shoe on the way up.

I was so thankful for you and felt so good that you both ended up together. I think it was a blessing on all sides. I thank you for all the love you all have given him over the years."

Writing the Pony story has been like putting together pieces of a jigsaw puzzle, or connecting the dots to a very complex picture. After getting in touch with Rebecca, who filled in many of the details from the early days when the pony first appeared, I phoned Steve, Rebecca's husband and Fred Backer's son. I was trying to recall that initial time when the vet came, a whole year after the pony first appeared on our property, and about 7 or 8 months since he was enclosed in our back yard. It was spring, and as we already mentioned earlier, we knew Pony needed his shots and to be seen by a vet. Steve was part of the gang who rounded him up.

The unedited phone conversation follows:

"Hi, Steve. We weren't sure when you all initially came with the vet. Was it the first Saturday in May? And can you recall which vet it was?"

"Right. I remember because the Kentucky Derby is always the first Saturday in May. You came to the farm to get my hay rope. You must have talked to my father first, and came over to the farm to pick up the rope. Okay, my father gave you my hay rope, I was in the tack room, and when I open the tack room door a nun - which is kind of out of place at the farm - walked in with my hay rope, I thought that was kind of an odd thing to see. You know, kind of hit me by surprise, right?" *(a short laugh)* "So then I asked my father what was going on, he said you're trying to catch that Pony - the one that Rebecca had purchased - and he goes on and says he told you we'd lend a hand if you needed us. So then about an hour later you called.

I went up there and it had to take us about four hours to finally catch that pony. We just kept running around and around, and then we finally caught him and Mary Beth "tranqed" him. Then Tony and Mary Beth worked on him, trimming his feet, and giving him all his vaccinations and his rabies shots and all that stuff. And I remember it was so funny because Mary Beth said, well, he's probably going to be under for only another couple of minutes. So hurry, to Tony, keep trimming him. I had my knee down on his neck, holding him and his head, holding him down, for when he came to. And I'll never forget when he did come to, he bit my shoe."

"I remember…"

"Yeah, and that's kind of an odd thing for a pony to do. So, I thought that was pretty amazing. And then basically that was it. So, then he came out of it. But I know it was Mary Beth and I know the guy's name was Tony. He's probably moved out of the area by now."

"Do you know if it was the first time they'd been here?"

"I'm sure it was. Yes, that was absolutely the first time that they captured the pony and anybody came, you know, to do anything with him. We did the same thing the next year, okay? In other words, the next year we came and caught him again and it only took half the amount of time to catch him then. I think you had better fencing and stuff like that. And we caught him, and gave him his shots."

"OK, this definitely is connecting the dots because that's the year then that Marne came, the other vet. Do you remember her?"

"Oh, that's right. It was Marne. I just couldn't remember which vet was there the second time. Okay…"

"but the first time it was Mary Beth…"

"…it was definitely Mary Beth, and it was definitely Tony."

"Right. So, Tony must have gotten in touch with you that second year and actually asked..."

"Yes, 'cause he was doin' work at our farm at that point."

"Did your Dad come the second time? And was it your nephew Derick?"

"Yes. He's my nephew."

"Thank you so much Steve."

"Anytime, let me know if you need anything else about it."

"All right, thank you. It's been a long time, but your memory is good. I too clearly recall him coming to, and swinging around with his head and getting you in the work boot. I remember that."

"He was quite feisty, quite feisty..."

"He never showed any kind of aggression like that ever again. But I think it was because your knee was on his neck!"

"Right, right. He was just trying to get me off. Yeah, that's what he was trying to do. I can't blame him for that."

"No, I can't either, because all the time the pony was here if anything he seemed scared of people. He was with us, you know, for 27 years. Can you believe that?"

"Yes, it's hard to believe it's been that long...

"That's pretty scary. Really, time flies, doesn't it?"

"Right. It does, it really does."

"Well, OK, thanks so much. You take care now, Steve."

"You too, Sister Margo. Thank you."

Backer Farm, Mendham New Jersey

Pony's story could not have happened without Steve's Dad, Fred Backer. Fred and his family were always there to help in the early days when the pony was first with us. Here is a photo of Fred on his beloved tractor.

"...kindred spirits."

Over the years the pony left such a lasting impression with so many people. Again and again, we'd hear similar stories, from guests at our retreat house, visitors, and others staying at the convent. Pony became a highlight when people came to visit us. Although he was still very shy, if he happened to be in one of his more mellow moods, over the years even a stranger could stroke his nose, or scratch his ears (which he loved.) We always reminded people when approaching him to move slowly and quietly, avoiding quick jerky motions. When kids came running over excitedly to meet the pony, it wasn't easy...

One unusual exception was a little girl named Emma. Her grandmother just happened to have a camera with her and captured a few delightful moments. Here are a few of them:

Janet was a woman who lived with us for a number of years. Sharing some of her memories might give a glimpse of the role the pony had with countless others. Let's see the unedited conversation Janet and I had one day while chatting in our sitting room:

"Janet, would you like to share some of your memories of the pony?"

"Okey-dokey, so as I remember it, I think Pony and I came to live here about the same time."

"And do you remember what year?"

"Well, I think I came to live here in '96.

"He arrived in '92."

"Okay, I came to visit. I used to come on the weekends and go back there, where Pony was. And I would sit just very quietly. And usually he would just graze, you know, around me. Sometimes when I went back there, he would nuzzle my back and lay his head on my shoulder. Usually my left shoulder."

"He would do that with a few of us. I'm curious, did you talk to him at all?"

"It was just sort of silent, no, we were silent together, because I was very depressed then, and sometimes I would cry."

"Do you think he sensed that?"

"Oh, yes. I know he sensed that. I know he sensed I had heavy stuff on my mind and he stayed near me. Whenever I went out there he stayed near me."

"So, I guess he had a ministry. Some people, you know, when we talk about him having a ministry, they look at us, kind of raising their eyebrows."

"Well, he definitely had a ministry to me… but he wouldn't let me touch him. No, he wouldn't let me touch him, you know, when he laid his head on my shoulder. I couldn't touch him. I couldn't move. I just had to be very, very still and allow him to do that, and not move. And we would stay that way for a while… as long as I didn't move… But the memory that I really hold is Easter, the Easter Sunday when your Mom died."

"It was 2016. Easter morning, March 27, 2016."

"I was up on the fourth floor, and I heard him whinny, long and loud, and I thought, oh my God, what is wrong with Pony because he was always quiet. And I came down and I looked out there where he was, and he was fine. And I asked somebody, did you hear Pony? And they said no, and I said he just let out the longest loud whinny. They didn't hear it."

"And what time do you think that was? Can you recall?"

"It was shortly after 9:30 in the morning because I had just heard the chapel bell ring. And then I heard that it was when your Mom died that he let out that whinny. And I thought, oh my God."

"I was with her at her side and that's when she took her last breath."

"Yes, I knew you weren't here, and I thought that she might have died."

"I always knew we had some kind of a connection, the pony and me. It sometimes was uncanny."

35

"Oh, yeah, and that certainly. And I thought, how could nobody not hear him? How could nobody not hear him because it was so loud. But I guess I was meant to hear that."

"Wonderful story... anything else come to mind?"

"Over the years. Mmm. I'm trying to think... Petie and Pony running around, running around the backyard. Oh, and when Pony got going, he was so handsome… he was really a handsome fella..."

"How he arched his neck, and his tail would flow behind him. Yes, he was a handsome fellow alright. Other times he'd whinny or neigh was when he was way out back grazing, and we'd show up with the dog. The pony would see Petie, letting out with this long whinny, and come running up to him."

"Oh, but that was different... that was a different sound."

"It was kind of excited, almost joyful..."

"What I heard on Easter was, was… it's hard to describe..."

"Was it sad or mournful?"

"Like I said, it's just hard to describe… and because I was upstairs, you know, up on the fourth floor, I couldn't hear it as clearly as if I'd been outside."

"The sisters would have been in Chapel during that time, at terce, or heading in that direction."

"Yes, they would have, you're right… so, there we have it…"

"Thanks, Janet…"

***

Now we'd like to share Dr. Marne Platt's memories of our boy. Although over the years we had numerous vets attend Pony, the one who really loved him was Dr. Marne, his first "primary physician." Unfortunately, she had to give up her practice as she was very allergic to horses. But over the years we kept in contact.

"The first time I remember hearing about the pony was when I was still working at the Califon Animal Hospital. I had been there for just a couple of months. I was a newly graduated veterinarian. A call came in that the pony at the local convent was lame; the receptionist, Pam, knew a bit of the story. She came back to the three veterinarians - Debbie, Marybeth, and me. We decided that I would go, and I think I went out on a Saturday morning.

That was also when I met you, Sister Margo, for the first time. I met the pony and heard a little bit more of his story, how he had been running loose around Mendham until he ran up onto the grounds of the convent and the nuns gave him sanctuary, which I thought was a great story.

37

He was beautiful, but obviously footsore and clearly needed his feet trimmed pretty badly. And he was a little bit foundered from all the fruit that was in the pasture. But we could not get near him at all, so I left a bottle of sedative granules to put in his food, and we planned to try again in a few days.

Of course, when I came back a few days later that hadn't worked at all and we still couldn't get near him. We had to come up with Plan B...

Plan B took a little bit of working out. We tried one more time with a bigger dose of the acepromazine granules, without success. Remember this was 1994, so a lot of the medications that we have now were not available then. But I'm not really sure it would have made a difference, because we still couldn't get near him! For all that he was footsore, he looked really happy. That was actually nice to see.

Anyway, I went off and we all called around to find some help. Someone - I don't remember whom - connected me with Tony, a local blacksmith who used to rope in the rodeo. He offered to come with some friends and some people from a local farm, and I think one of the lay associates from the convent helped us too.

We arrived with a whole group of people on a beautiful Saturday morning to begin this adventure. It started with a few of us going into the pasture and Tony trying to rope him. That started the *real* rodeo because he ran around that big back yard for about two hours! We could not get a rope on him.

I really think he was having a great time; his ears were up and he was jumping up and down off the different levels of pasture. Every time Tony would toss the rope and it looked like it was just going to settle right over his neck, the pony would duck his head, it would fall off to the side and off he would go again.

At one point he even tried to run me over, and sent me flying, I could swear as he went by that he was laughing at us.

So it was kind of funny, we were all in a good mood and thought it was hilarious. In the background we could hear the sisters praying, because this was going on for several hours. It was pretty amusing!

Finally, after a couple of hours, when I guess Pony was a little tired and we were all *very* tired, Tony was able to get a rope over his head. We put it around a tree and then let him run himself in circles until he was standing up next to the tree.

Then I was able to get right up next to him and give him some medication so that he would first be a little bit sedated, and then we could finally make him unconscious.

It was quite funny; all the time that he was running around he looked a lot bigger than he actually was... I mean, I'm only 5 feet tall, and by the time I got next to him when he was standing still, he looked a lot smaller than he had when he'd tried to run me over. Lots of things about the pony were a little surprising...

The next surprise was how much anesthetic it took for him to lie down and go to sleep. I ended up giving this little guy, who couldn't have weighed more than 350 or 400 pounds, as much medication as it took to anesthetize a draft horse that weighs closer to 1500 or 1700 pounds. So it took a *lot* of medication to make him go to sleep.

He finally did lie down like a good boy and Tony was able to trim his feet. I gave him all of his vaccines, because we didn't think he had had any in a long time, and a very thorough exam. He had a very strong heart that was pumping away. We cleaned him up in various places and just generally took care of him while he was sleeping.

Of course, he tried to wake up halfway through, so that required more medication to help him go back to sleep.

Finally, when we were finished, we let him wake up. He woke up very quickly, but was very smart. When he woke up, he sat on his chest with his front legs stuck out, and I guess he waited for the world to stop moving around him. He stood up kind of slowly, looked at us, and then just trotted away to stand under a tree like nothing had happened, happy as a clam. That was really good to see!

Afterwards, the lemonade you gave us was, I think, the best thing I had ever tasted in my life.

So the day was really successful. The whole thing probably took us about four hours by the time we got there, did what we had to, and cleaned everything up.

After the first adventure was so successful, coming in to rope Pony in the spring or early summer became an annual event that we all looked forward to. We would just come in and plan to spend a few hours, maybe in the early afternoon, chasing him around, getting our exercise, and finally getting him to lie down. I still think he always had a ton of fun, because there was never a moment when he turned shy or nasty, or had his ears back. He was always ears up, running all over the place, jumping up and down, running between us, zigzagging... he was really cute and I think he was having a great time. I always thought he was laughing at us.

But it did get to be something that I wondered about. How long could we keep doing this? I used to try to help him settle down, or at least, that was my plan. It never really worked.

On days when I wasn't working, or if I was up in the area and had time to take a lunch break, I would come to the convent and just sit in the back yard with Pony. I'd sit under one of the trees and read and maybe eat a sandwich, and try to get him to take some carrots or lettuce from my hand.

I think that worked once over a few years.

He really could tell, I think, that I was the one chasing him around, even if he enjoyed it. I could sit and watch him. I could sit there for a couple of hours, and he would eventually come down and sniff around me. But I could never touch him. He would not let me get near him.

You could have knocked me over with a feather when, a

couple of years later, I heard that he had actually consented to wear a halter. I thought that showed a lot of time and patience with him, because he was determined not to let anybody get close to him at all.

I continued coming to visit even after I left Califon Animal Hospital and moved to Montclair, N.J. Eventually I moved to North Carolina at the end of 1998 and to Europe in 2005. But every time I was back in New Jersey I would try to come in and visit.

The last time I saw Pony was in 2010 or 2011. I was in New Jersey for a business trip, so I came to visit. I walked the labyrinth with Mother Suzanne and of course I visited Pony, and he came closer. I heard that people could touch him, but I think he remembered me, and he looked at me kind of sideways. He came up close and he sniffed, but I couldn't pet him like I wanted to. But it was good just to talk to him, and to know that other people could touch him.

The rest of my connections with Pony would come from writing. When you were still sending out printed newsletters there was always a column, "A Letter From Pony" or from Pony and Petie. I loved those. There were always great pictures of him and he had - or you, writing in his voice had - such a calm and easy perspective on life. I still have those newsletters saved in a box in storage. And of course, he was written up in the local paper, and I think I still have a copy of that too.

Pony is one of my favorite practice stories, so people all over the world have heard about him and seen his picture. He was just so much fun and so special. He really made practice special for me, particularly as a new veterinarian. I think he made Community of St. John Baptist a more special place too. He certainly made it a fun place to visit, and just to see what was going on.

Roberta Shields was mentioned earlier in the book, the woman who saw the Daily Record article. I asked her if she would like to share some of her thoughts and memories.

"My best recollection is that I first heard about Pony in October of 1992 when the Daily Record did an article about him and his arrival at the Convent, and that donations were being sought to build a fence and a shed for his protection. My Mother and I sent in a very small donation. Soon thereafter we received a thank you note from Sister Margo and a print of the photo that appeared in the newspaper article. The photo was breathtaking. It had been taken by Daily Record photographer Chris Pedota.

Personally, I think his photograph of Sr. Margo and Pony is a masterpiece! The setting is magnificent, the lighting inspiring and the message it transmits so important. It shows mutual two-way respect, humility, kindness, generosity, compassion, communication, tolerance and trust - all without words and in a setting that is unmatched in its beauty.

That powerful photo has so much to teach us about the beings with whom we share the planet and how that knowledge should shape our actions. Its peaceful setting belies the urgency with which what it teaches should be used for change. Pony in his wisdom made it possible for the photographer to capture that moment. Without Pony and all the miracles that he embodies, and the artistic eye of the photographer, that priceless moment, and many others, would have been lost.

Back then, I was just beginning to try my hand at painting, and as a life-long animal lover, I chose animals as my subjects. As any self-taught painter knows, you go through stages. Little by little you tackle new and more difficult things. I'd not yet tackled any kind of landscape, never painted a horse or a person, and never painted anything larger than 8 x 10.

But I was so stunned by the beauty of that photograph that all that was about to change. I wanted to try painting the scene in that photo. It took me two or three months to complete.

Once it was done, I reached out to the Convent to tell them my plan. I hoped to enter the painting in an upcoming local Art show in Livingston and if it sold, to donate the proceeds to Pony. And if it did not sell, maybe they would like to have it? Before sharing those plans, I first contacted the photographer, knowing that the amazing image that he had captured was his, not mine. I wanted his Ok to proceed, an Ok which he generously gave.

Fortunately, which I say now with hindsight, the painting did not sell! So, I called the Convent and asked if I could bring it to them. They said yes. My Mother and I were invited to join the sisters for late afternoon tea and to bring the painting. Here we were, two non-church going strangers coming to give them a painting, a painting by a very amateur painter, that they had not seen and that no one else wanted to buy! Regardless, we could not have been more warmly welcomed, as, I should add, has been the case in all the years and visits that have followed. I remember being so impressed too at the time by the presence of an elderly straggly shepherd mix dog that walked in on us that day. That was another of many clues that these people in this place were kindred spirits that genuinely cared about animals, human and non-human alike.

Had Pony not selected CSJB as his sanctuary, I doubt that I would have ever visited the Convent or met his caretakers or his friends. Nor would I have been on the receiving end of the enormous comfort the sisters generously extended to me several years later during my own loss of a loved one.

My friendship with the sisters and Pony began when he arrived in 1992 and continues even now that he is gone. Their story is, in and of itself, an inspiration to all who know it. It provides a message of hope and faith in doing what is right that is as strong as that in any story ever told. Like other great stories, it too played out in the lives of humble souls seeking peace and safety who were fortunate enough to find those doing good for others with no fanfare and no expectations in return. By the grace of God, Pony found his way to the Convent. And thanks to God, the sisters allowed him to stay and gave him the best of care. In that shining moment the world became a better place, not just for his own 27 years there, but for the lifetimes of all who know his story and have come to trust, respect and love him. He will always be both a blessing and an inspiration. Simple gestures of love and kindness, gentle care, persistence and respect can change the world."

"...close encounter with a bear."

The rodeo days came to an end. Quite frankly, we did not feel comfortable with the event, worried that the pony might injure himself or have a heart attack. He seemed to know when the vet was coming and just took right off into the back pasture.

As an aside, it took a few years before the pony allowed any of us to touch him. Mind you, he had to be in the right mood, "mellowed out" as they say. Although, thinking back now, it worked both ways. Speaking softly to him always helped, and I often would sing to him. If anyone approached him too impatiently or aggressively, he just wouldn't let them near him.

When we sat down somewhere out in his territory and waited patiently, he just might walk over. Occasionally if I sat motionless, he'd approach me and rest his head on my shoulder. If I lowered my head, he sometimes leaned forward and put his forehead against the top of my head. We'd be like that for several minutes. Truly a very special moment. Time seemed to stand still. It would not happen if I had a lot on my mind and the brain was racing - you know, the hamster on the wheel. It only was effective by quieting the mind, slowing down thoughts, having no expectations, just being very present to the moment...

One day I reached out toward him - with the palm facing downwards and the back of the hand up - and he tentatively touched it with his nose. Very slowly I turned my hand upwards and slid my fingers under his chin, and gently began scratching him. Gradually over time he could be touched more and more, but only if he made the first move. Any quick motion on our part and he'd jerk his head away. As the years went by, he began to trust more, so others could also touch him - only of course if he was ready. We had to know if he was in one of his mellow moods or not.
It was always on his terms...

46

Pony had quite a personality as you no doubt have already seen. Let's share some more anecdotal stories that we hope you will enjoy…

Earlier in the book we mentioned how the pony would sometimes impatiently push his rubber bowl toward us with his nose when we came out to feed him, especially on a cold night. Well, after some time, if we said, "give me your bowl… get your bowl" he would obligingly put his head down and push the bowl toward the fence where we were standing. It happened so frequently after a while that he just did it without being asked. So smart.

Occasionally we'd give our boy an extra apple or carrot as a treat, broken up into several pieces. In his inimitable way, he might try grab it from our hand with his mouth in a rough manner. If we said "easy" or "be gentle" he would respond accordingly. He seemed to understand what we were saying. If he thought we had a treat in our pocket, he might nudge us rather roughly. Horses don't know how strong they are! Those magic words "be gentle" and "easy" worked like a charm. Well, usually…

Often if the apple wasn't cut in pieces, if we held it out toward him, he would simply take a bite out of it while we were holding it. Needless to say, care was given to be sure our fingers were out of the way!

On occasion if the pony was in one of his mellow moods, I couldn't resist leaning over and giving him a kiss on his nose. I'd often say something like, "little boy, can I give you a kiss?" and then proceed to plant one on the top of his nose. In time that evolved to bending down toward him, saying, "give me a kiss," and he promptly pushed his nose against the side of my face. Sweet, oh so sweet...

The sisters wear habits, as most of you know, and around our waists we wear what's called a "cincture," or what could be considered a rope-like belt. The cincture is part of a traditional habit, going back centuries. On the "rope" are knots representing the three vows we take when life professed (poverty, chastity and obedience.) The cincture is secured in place by yet another larger knot, on the side.

If you recall our boy did not like anything that resembled a halter or a rope. Several times over the years if I happened to be sitting out back with the pony, he would attempt to loosen the one larger knot with his teeth, very deliberately. At first this behavior was rather curious, and I wondered what he was doing. But it finally occurred to me... he was trying to "set me free."

***

Our property spans about 65 acres, consisting of several buildings, lawns, gardens, fruit trees, cedars, evergreens and a variety of deciduous trees. The surrounding area is made up of woodlands, providing a perfect habitat for a variety of wildlife... birds, rabbits, chipmunks, deer, squirrels, raccoons, foxes, coyotes... and occasionally bears.

So, let's take a moment now to recall a particular visit from one of our black bears.

Richard, our estate manager at the time, set out as he always did to give the pony his breakfast. But Pony was not up by his fence where he usually was at that hour in

48

the morning, waiting anxiously to be fed. Something caught Rich's attention. He could hear the pony snorting, making quite a stir, and finally could see him way down in the back, near one of the summer houses. When Rich looked more closely, he suddenly realized the pony was not alone...

A black bear was within feet of our boy.

Rich came into the house looking for one of us so we could go check on what was happening. He found Sr. Linda Clare, so they walked out back together. When they got closer, in Sr Linda Clare's words, "it became very obvious that Pony WAS IN CHARGE!!!" He was snorting and keeping the bear at bay. And then the bear went further into the corner by the trees. Pony continued to snort, and at one point when the bear got a little too close, the pony "whirled and kicked at him."

Linda Clare continues, "It was after that when the bear 'gave in' and the pecking order was established - Pony in charge, and the bear second."

Ever so slowly, the pony began to head in the direction of the front enclosure where he knew his breakfast was there waiting for him. And would you know the bear was right behind? Not too close, mind you. If the pony stopped, the bear followed suit, waiting patiently for our boy to continue, "one time rolling, one time sitting, and then lying down."

At last Pony made it to his fence and started eating his breakfast, the bear not too far away, just behind the dumpster. And again, in Linda Clare's words, "The bear then stuck his nose out toward Pony, and Pony stuck his nose out to the bear, and there was probably less than 6 feet separating their noses."

Our bruin eventually decided to leave, making his way toward the woods. It was certainly an exciting day, to say the least.

Occasionally someone saw Pony rear up at something, and we assumed it was just another bear out there.

Years later, one of our short-term residents was walking in from her car in the parking lot. She saw a bear, over by the dumpster, near the garage. Apparently, the woman was quite startled, and walking quickly back to her car, waited it out to see what might happen. The bear slowly made his way past her car towards the woods, seemingly totally oblivious of her sitting there in the car (so it appeared... or, he could have just been ignoring her as he'd done to some of us!) The experience undoubtedly left quite an impression on the woman, as it was her first "close encounter" with a black bear.

But within a few weeks another bear was spotted, this time much younger and smaller. Subsequently, the woman named our two frequent visitors "Sherman" (for Sherman tank) and the smaller one, "Cooper" (for mini Cooper.)

Just a quick comment about our bears here in New Jersey. There's been a lot of controversy over the issue of hunting them. The convent has about 65 acres in Mendham, and another small property up in West Milford bordering the Norvin Green State Forest. Over the years we've had the opportunity of seeing many bears at both locations, and never noted aggressive behavior that could be considered harmful or dangerous. Admittedly, they can be a nuisance when they knock down the bird feeders!

Nevertheless, we still love our bears...

"…this little guy never ceased to amaze us."

An important fall ritual or tradition we've continued over the years is the Blessing of the Animals. October 4th is recognized worldwide as the feast of St. Francis, or simply St. Francis day. Francis loved all animals, and was known to have practiced his preaching to the birds! Churches everywhere will have a service, inviting people to bring their pets to receive a blessing. The Cathedral of Saint John the Divine in NYC has continued their blessing of the animals, and over the years have had some very unique participants attend. On more than one occasion an elephant led the procession up the steps into the Cathedral to be blessed at the high altar.

Well, our service is definitely scaled down, yet in our eyes no less important! We have our own cherished event every year, inviting our neighbors and friends to bring their beloved furry companions. We never know who will show up.

One particular year Karen and her family brought their menagerie - a horse, a pony, two dogs and a cat. When we rounded up our dog, cat and pony, by the time the service began, it was a veritable three ring circus…

Once all our four-legged participants get sorted out, the humans are given a small printed program that has some prayers on it. Even the pony tried to read what was on the page...

Everyone receives a blessing and a dousing of holy water. Sr. Barbara Jean is attempting to sprinkle Pony with the holy water, but as you can see, he wants nothing to do with it...

Each season had its joys as well as it's challenges, always presenting certain situations that required our attention. But it also provided the opportunity to spend quality time with our boy. As time went on, he became more trusting and interacted with us more frequently.

With the onset of autumn, the flies disappeared, but the fruit trees on our property were another issue. One year we had a bumper crop of pears and we had to remove them from his enclosure - wheelbarrows full of them. (Pony can tell you about that himself later in the book in one of the newsletter "columns".) And then there were the apples. That was resolved by fencing off the apple orchard so our boy couldn't get to them. He wasn't at all happy about that... but there was always an apple or two that rolled over near enough to him so he could get it.

Fall inevitably brought another annoying problem. We had to deal with burrs. We knew autumn had arrived when the pony appeared from his large back enclosure, literally covered with the nasty clinging things imbedded in his forelock and mane, and sometimes on his face, his legs, and chest.

Sr. Mary Lynne taking burrs off our boy

Some of us would spend a lot of time with the pony, laboriously removing the burrs, one by one. It became a yearly ritual, to be sure. Pony would just stand there patiently while we were working on him. He seemed to know what we were doing. We found an old brush used for blow drying hair, and it proved quite effective when he was so matted.

Ryan (the estate manager's son) would "walk the fences" out back on a regular basis checking to see if any were down or needed mending. He was the one who noticed a lot of the burrs growing in amongst the other weeds along the periphery of the property. He suggested going around and just pulling the burrs up. It seemed to make a difference... thanks, Ryan.

By the time autumn moved on toward the colder months, Pony had grown a thick winter coat. He was so cute. He reminded us of one of those Steiff stuffed animals. As he grew to trust us more, we could run our fingers through his luxurious coat. It was almost 2 inches thick. Although it might be frigid outside, you could feel how warm his body temperature was underneath.

Snow didn't appear to phase our boy in the least. He seemed to like it. But on the paths where he walked regularly, the snow became packed down, changing to solid ice. Quite frankly when that happened it was cause for concern to say the least, so we either spread sand or scattered old hay over the area.

One time I happened to look out from the window and saw him very carefully walking along the base of the evergreens where the ground was slightly raised, making his way to the fence. By doing this he avoided the ice altogether. That little guy never ceased to amaze us.

Another winter concern was Pony's hooves getting impacted with snow that turned into solid ice. But we learned when his body heat became elevated, the ice and anything else mixed in (hay, pine shavings, etc.) would drop out. If we gave him extra hay in his shed, we'd find innumerable hard clumps of oval ice "pancakes" scattered around in there amongst the old hay and bedding.

During the winter months a submersible heating element was placed in the pony's water basin, keeping the water at room temperature so it wouldn't freeze. It also helped to warm our little guy's insides, to be sure. Well, the pony learned that if he took his foreleg and plunked his foot in the tepid water, the warmth would dissolve the ice that was caked in his hoof. We couldn't believe it when we saw him do it. Again, smart boy…

Of course, it meant Ryan had to clean his water basin much more frequently!

When we had those terrific snowstorms, we'd run a long extension cord out to his shed and would hook up a heated water bucket in there. It also generated a little warmth. In those winter months as already mentioned we'd usually give him his hay in his shed, supplemented with his senior pellets. He had everything he needed right there, with all the comforts of home sweet home...

A remaining winter problem was solved by placing some insulation at the top of the shed where there was a gap of about 5 inches between the roof and the top of the walls. Before we did that, a lot of the warmth generated from Pony's body heat wouldn't stay within the shed. Heat rises!

Several times during the 27 years our boy was with us we had blizzard-like conditions that dumped almost 3 feet of snow. He always seemed undaunted even in those conditions. (Pony talks later about these winters in several of his newsletter columns "Pony's Point of View.")

He loved to "snack" on the hedgerow behind the convent. Although we gave him plenty to eat, lest we forget, he was still a foraging beast!

Once the winter was past, Pony's thick coat would start to come out, and often in clumps. In the early days when we couldn't get too near him, we let nature take its sweet course, and by summer his coat was sleek and shiny. He just loved to roll in an area where there was either mud or dirt, yes, truly dirt, not earth... or on occasion, grass.

With some observation on our part, there were some other ways he was able to rid himself of all that hair, as well as groom himself. We'd see him push his body along the hedgerow, rubbing up against the bushes, combing his tail out, and dealing with his winter coat.

In the later years we were able to use a tool called a "shredding blade" which efficiently did a great job in removing Pony's winter coat (thanks to Jeanie for giving it to us.) And he loved to be brushed, but of course had to be in the right mood. Being that it was the spring when the birds were preparing for their little families, we'd often save the hair so the birds could use it for building their nests.

It's good to recycle...

With the advent of spring comes the rain. So often we'd find our boy way out back during one of those steady showers in April, and there he would be, standing in the middle of his pasture, eyes half closed, the rain pouring down on him. It must have felt so good.

And of course, spring means fresh green grass, to the pony's delight. But we learned if new grass is eaten too quickly, it will most likely cause the horse to founder, especially ponies. That first spring he started limping, so we became very concerned. Just as we suspected, it was from the fresh new grass that was so full of nutrients. We learned to control how long he was grazing, as well as cut back on his sweet feed. As the years progressed, we discontinued the sweet feed altogether and went to a balanced diet of hay supplemented with pellets.

April and May inevitably brought the tiny gnats or "no-see-ums," those persistent little buggers that would get into his ears, sometimes leaving crusty dried blood. We found something called SWAT, an antiseptic salve that was also a repellent, and very soothing. Eventually, Pony allowed me to clean out his ears with warm water on a paper towel, then apply the SWAT in his ears. It also was effective on any scratches or minor cuts he'd get on his knees. Great stuff.

Summer came with its challenges which was primarily the flies. Somewhere we heard that Avon Skin So Soft diluted with water was a good alternative to chemical insect repellents. It worked wonders when sprayed on

our boy. And it also is effective for us humans as well...
why not give it a try?

But it was those awful horse flies that drove Pony crazy.
Sometimes we'd see him run from his grazing way out
back, heading directly for his shed. At first, we could not
understand this behavior until we then realized he was
fleeing from the horse flies (apparently horse flies don't
like going into enclosed areas like sheds or barns.) Once
again, smart boy...

One last issue we had in any season was the chronic
problem with his eyes. The vet provided an antibiotic
ointment when his eyes got red or infected, and the pony
would allow me to apply the ointment. In the later years,
he'd stand there and close his eye while it was being
administered.

Our wild pony had come a long way from those early
years. There were moments where he acted almost
normal!

"...his non-human friends and companions."

A significant part of Pony's life that we cannot possibly leave out were his non-human friends and companions. As mentioned earlier, most of the woodland creatures would drink from Pony's water basin all year 'round - in winter it wouldn't not freeze. Birds, squirrels, foxes, coyotes, bears, chipmunks, racoons... Oh, if we only thought of putting up a night cam recorder.

Sometimes we'd look out and see a deer under the overhang to his shed, the pony close by. We weren't sure if it was one of his girlfriends. Many of the deer would often be helping themselves to the trace mineral salt lick.

Most of us living here love nature and appreciate the diversity all around us. The deer come to visit all the time. We saw a few the other day out under the overhang to Pony's shed. And we've kept the water basin for all the wildlife, even in the winter months.

Only just recently we had an unexpected visitor. Several of our sisters were clustered in the kitchen looking out the windows at something. And there, peering in the window, was a wild turkey on the roof of the carport. She was watching the other birds on the feeder very intently, trying to figure out how to get to it. The following day the feeder was on the ground, totally destroyed. Oh dear, she must have landed on It, unaware of her rather large size.

Henrietta (as we named her) remained with us for about a week, outstaying her welcome. Although many of us had grown quite fond of her, we thought it better for Henrietta to be in her natural habitat. So with some difficulty, she was encouraged to go into a large dog crate we found in the house somewhere. Ken then transported our turkey far out into the woods, in a wheel barrel...
She returned a few days later.

61

Appearing to be reading the sign by the Pony's fence that we never bothered to remove, Henrietta seems to be thinking. It says, "You can love me, but please don't feed me." Hm...

Our feathered guest was getting all too comfortable living in our backyard. At night she flew up into the trees over the garages. She had everything she needed - food, shelter, and water.

But Henrietta had become quite a nuisance.

After days of frustration on our part, our cook Leo offered to take our turkey to another location, a lovely small lake bordering a wooded area, miles away. So, after luring her a second time into the dog crate, Henrietta was carefully placed into the back of his truck and transported to her new habitat.

As many of you probably thought, just as we did, it isn't often when you see a solitary turkey. They are usually part of a flock with other similar like-minded creatures. Perhaps she had belonged to someone? Who knows...

Prayers for Henrietta as she begins her new life in a setting where we hope she'll find other "birds of the same feather..."

Most of you reading this have known the community a long time and are very familiar with all our furry four-legged residents who lived with us over the years. They all were "rescues" from different shelters or foster homes.

We thought you'd all like to read about our beloved menagerie! And we hope the stories and sketches will bring back some wonderful memories for you.

We'll begin with our dear Pucker...

Pucker

Pucker was already in residence when Pony arrived in 1992. Having come here around 1983, she was a "rescue" from a shelter in Pennsylvania. Pucker was quite shy, but a "very serious watch dog," always letting us know if something was amiss. She would sit in a strategic spot under the huge Oregon pine out in front where she could look down our road, always vigilant...

Being a Beagle and Shepherd mix, Pucker's bark changed depending on the circumstances. When running through the woods, she'd let out with a high-pitched Beagle yelp, especially when in pursuit of a rabbit or a squirrel. But when she was "guarding the house" her bark was distinctly a Shepherd's, deep and very ferocious.

Our sweet girl left us for heavenly realms in the fall of 1996. She had a good life living with us...

In the following spring we knew it was time for another dog. Our Superior at the time, Sr. Suzanne Elizabeth, had a few stipulations: that the dog be a female (as they tend to stay near home and don't wander); is older than 1 ½ years old; and is about 35 or 40 lbs.

I offered to make a few calls, the first being St. Hubert's Giralda, being sure to give the above details to the person on the other end of the phone. She said she thought they had just the right dog for us, suggesting we drive over. Not wasting any time, Sr. Mary Lynne and I took off to St. Hubert's, only about 25 minutes away. After a staff person greeted us, we were ushered to a waiting room with a number of chairs around the periphery, and invited to take a seat. A door opened and out bounded a beautiful black and white Border Collie and Springer mix, still damp from getting a bath. He came right over to us, wagging his tail, and then proceeded to back into me, promptly sitting down on my feet. He was about 50 lbs., and just over a year old. His name was Petie. Sr. Mary Lynne fell in love with this guy from the start (as did I.) But I kept thinking about the very clear instructions we had from our dear Superior; female, 35 pounds, older than a year and a half.

They were about to close for the day, so we left saying we'd give them a call. As we were heading out to the parking lot, a woman with her son were heading toward the building, and Mary Lynne said, "there goes Petie." Oh dear, we had to move fast... walking very quickly, almost running, we returned to the building, went to the front desk and asked if we could borrow their phone to call home (don't forget, those were the days before cell phones.) We then poured out to Sr. Suzanne Elizabeth all about Petie. Needless to say, she was not too thrilled about the news, but agreed to give him a trial period.

We drove back to Mendham with our new dog in the car, sitting on Mary Lynne's lap the whole way (I was driving, don't worry...)

Petie was a character, to say the least. It would take almost another book to tell his "tale", but let's share some highlights, as most of you reading this must love animal stories.

Petie

It was shortly after Easter when Petie arrived, and he was allowed free access throughout the entire house. Following tradition, the Paschal Candle was standing in St. Michaels chapel, our little chapel on the second floor. And all around the Candle were lovely plants that formed the Paschal Garden. Now Petie had never seen anything like this, and apparently just assumed it was like any other garden. Uh huh, you got it. He proceeded to lift his leg, watering the plants very thoroughly before anyone could stop him.

A few more times this behavior was repeated until one day one of us happened to be in the basement. Just as she was opening a door down there, Petie was caught in the act - watering the corner of the door. All it took was the loud noise of the door slamming and a little scolding him at the time. It never happened again…

Petie liked to go exploring if he got loose outside. One day a few of us looked out our window, and a red sports car convertible pulled up in front of the convent building.

At the wheel driving was a pretty blond woman, and next to her in the passenger's seat, sitting tall and very handsome, was... Petie.

A few months later someone else pulled up in front, with our boy in his car. The man just happened to be an animal behaviorist who worked especially with dogs. He offered to give us some lessons to help train Petie, and we accepted (not really sure if the lessons were for the dog, or for us...)

One of our devoted associates offered to pay for an electric fence. It helped, but Petie was known to run right through it. He was incorrigible.

Petie was just so lovable we all put up with his antics, especially the pony. They were the best of friends...

As an aside, we'd like to say something about our CSJB community newsletter that came out about three times a year. All of our furry four-legged companions who were in permanent residence each wrote a "column" that also included some wonderful photographs. Reprints of the pony's column "Pony's Point of View" appear later in the book, and the pony talks quite a bit about Petie. We hope you'll take the time to read them.

We might mention that when he first got here, we noticed something wasn't quite right with Petie's sight. Indeed, he had to have surgery in both eyes due to an early onset of cataracts. The procedure was expensive, but another one of our dear associates offered to pay for the entire cost.

We cannot possibly thank enough all the friends and associates who have been so generous with their donations over the years. Our gratitude is more than you'll ever know...

About 5 years after Petie arrived, two other dogs came to live with us for a while. They didn't really get to know the pony as much as Petie did, although every so often we'd walk them back to the fence and they'd touch noses.

Let's first introduce you to Samantha, a Westie (West Highland Terrier) who had belonged to my cousin Chrissy who passed away very unexpectedly. My other cousin Diane, her sister, phoned my mom and asked if she could take Sam. My mother wasn't quite sure if she could handle a very bright energetic little dog, as she was already in her late 80's. So, we agreed to share the responsibility for Samantha's care, Sam spending part of the week with my mom, and the rest of the week with the sisters. Miss Samantha (as we also called her) was also quite a character. A book could be written about her as well. Perhaps another time...

We'd like to introduce you now to Mandy, a senior blond Golden/Lab mix who belonged to Sr. Mary Lynne's Dad. After Mary Lynne's father passed away, we gave Mandy a home.

Mandy

The two of them were great friends, often playing together.

Both girls, Sam and Mandy, stayed on the second floor in the convent, a space with numerous bedrooms and a few offices.

Just to keep the peace, the door at the end of the floor was always kept shut. Jack our cat was in residence at the time. Terriers and cats have a long history of not exactly getting along.

But Petie was allowed to join the girls whenever he wanted to come for a visit. He totally ignored them both.

When all three dogs were present, the second-floor wing could have passed as a kennel, to be sure...

But just for off the record, those of us humans who reside on that floor just happen to love dogs, so we all coexist very happily.

Suzanne Elizabeth and Sam taking their daily vitamins

In the subsequent years that followed, all three of our beloved dog companions crossed over the well-known Rainbow Bridge. The one sad thing about having "pets" is that they don't live as long as humans do. If you noticed, the word pets is placed in quotes. They mean so much more to most of us, and referring to them merely as pets truly doesn't seem to be adequate. They become part of our lives just as any other member of a family.

Petie left this earth in the spring of 2011. We think he had a stroke at the end. He was 16 years old, having lived a very full and happy life.

Our sweet Jennie came to us about six months later…

We found Jennie on Facebook, at a fostering place called Paula's Doghouse. A "rescue" from North Carolina, along with other puppies and dogs, our little girl was 13 weeks old when she arrived in October 2011.

If Jennie was out back by Pony's fence, she always kept him at a safe distance, yet occasionally they would touch noses like the others. She clearly did not want to get too close. She respected him, because after all, Pony was a lot bigger than she was!

When Jennie was a puppy, she would occasionally get into trouble. As you can see, she loved playing with yarn. Oh, and what a mess she made...

Our little girl is quite grown up now, and indeed takes her job very seriously. Her hearing is truly amazing, and of course she has to let us know if she thinks something should be brought to our attention.

A typical moment for Jennie, always listening...

"...our wonderful collection of furry felines."

By now, you cat lovers are probably wondering about our feline residents. Many of you already know that there has always been a cat and a dog living with us, at least during the years Pony was here.

There is a purpose for having both. Each has a very important job to do. The cats discourage mice (God forbid) or any renegade chipmunks possibly in the house. The canine in residence listens for any questionable sounds that could possibly threaten the welfare of the sisters (an unwelcome intruder.) And of course, if the doorbell rings, the dog will gladly provide the inevitable barking. Sigh.

Now, if we are being truthfully honest, the real reason for having our sweet furry companions is that all the sisters living here are softies for animals. It's been said upon occasion that one of the prerequisites for becoming a member of our community is that you love dogs, cats, birds, or any other wildlife that happen to enter the realm of our existence.

Frideswide was here when the pony first arrived in 1992, originally a stray from the nearby woods. She lived in the basement on a soft bed on a shelf in the copy room, and she loved watching the birds... We put a "cat-flap" in a window, level with the ground so she could come and go as she pleased. Sr. Deborah Francis was one of her caretakers.

Some months after Frideswide "crossed over," a few sisters drove over to St. Hubert's and found Patches. She was really Pony's favorite, as she would spend a lot of time out there with him. The two of them would "hang out" together in the pony's enclosure.

Patches

Sometimes we'd see Patches sitting on one of the fence posts, not far from Pony. She would often keep him company while he was eating his hay. Occasionally we'd see her walking around his feet while he was eating, brushing up against his fetlocks. The pony didn't seem to mind at all...

Patches was the first cat to have complete access to the house, so Petie took full advantage of that. Often they'd be tearing through the building, with Petie in hot pursuit. Now, the only command Petie ever obeyed was "sit." One of the sisters who happened to be nearby called out the magical word. Our boy promptly sat down, continuing to slide down the length of the hallway from the forward momentum of the chase. Ah, the quiet religious life…

Sadly, the time had come for Patches to cross over the Rainbow Bridge. The pony talks about noticing that his sweet friend hadn't been around for a while (see "Pony's Point of View" Sept 2002.)

And again we waited the usual length of time before considering another cat. Spring arrived, so once more off to St. Hubert's. This time we did have a few ground rules, the most important being whatever cat we brought home had to be able to hold his own with dogs.

Jack

Jack was a sweetie, and even the sisters who were allergic to cats loved him. He liked being around people, and often could be found in the office of our business manager. When Mary was working at her computer, Jack would be on her desk, "helping."

Jack did enjoy his naps.

A little anecdotal story about him. Although our Jack was such a love, he was also quite the hunter. One day he proudly brought a chipmunk into the house that was very much alive. It ended up on the 4th floor where Janet lived. She was away at the time, and upon returning found a chipmunk's nest in a basket of clean laundry.

Our Jack was with us for well over 10 years. He moved on to go to celestial realms in January 2014.

Once more we respected the appropriate interim before looking for another cat. This time we began searching online for another furry feline companion, hoping once again for a cat that was comfortable with dogs.

Bob was originally a rescue, then placed in a foster home that had both dogs and cats.

Our Bob was unusual. We thought he might be part Manx as he had no tail. If you read about Manx personalities, it was quite possible. They are intelligent, friendly, affectionate, and devoted to their family. It is said they are more like dogs than cats!

Bob was the unofficial greeter over at our retreat house, welcoming people as they arrived. He loved being outside, and often would not come in when we wanted. Jennie, following her herding instincts (we think she has some Border Collie in her,) would willingly oblige when we said, "go get Bob." She would immediately run to him, pin him down with her two front paws, and hold him there until we could go pick him up. It was a game.

Jennie and Bob were really great pals...

Bob was with us for only 3 years. One cold November day he never returned. We searched for him for days, but to no avail. We were all heartbroken.

Our next cat was from the Randolph Animal Shelter, Clara Elizabeth. The name she came with was Betty, and we thought that did not quite fit her. Originally, Clara was from the streets of Elizabeth. Hence how her new name evolved.

When our sweet girl first arrived, she was living on the fourth floor with Janet. She needed a lot of care early on, as she had just been spayed. She also had the "sniffles" and ear mites.

In time, our little Clara evolved to a lovely young lady as you can see…

After Janet left, Sr Deborah Francis spent some time up on the fourth floor to keep Clara company, but as the days and weeks went by, we thought we'd let her explore the rest of the house.

We often find Miss Clara in the sitting room.

As did most of our furry feline friends, Clara loves watching the birds on the feeders.

The birds just continue doing whatever they are doing, totally ignoring the cat's presence.

Bob watching the birds

The last member of our feline collection is Kooky, who began her life on the streets of NYC. Kooky is very shy, and her personality is, well… different. She lived with our sisters for nearly 11 years at the Mission house of the Church of St. Mary the Virgin on West 46th Street.

The sisters returned to Mendham in 2018, and Kookie was allowed to come with them, now living on the 3rd floor. She has always been attached to Sr. Laura Katharine and is often found hiding under Sister's scapular while she works on her computer.

We love our furry companions, as well as our sweet feathered friends. Each has a ministry to all those who come here.

"...what took you so long? I've been waiting."

All the years Pony was with us, although I was primarily responsible for him, thank God we had a team who helped care for our boy. Whoever the estate manager was at the time would do the 8:30am and 4:30pm feedings during the week. We were so grateful to have Ken McCurdy, our estate manager from 2005 to the present, and his son Ryan. Weekends and holidays were covered by the sisters.

In the later years we added a third "snack" in the evening, around 8:15 pm, and that was usually yours truly. If I was away leading a group to Ireland or the UK, Sr. Suzanne Elizabeth or Sr. Mary Lynne would cover for me on those late feedings. On very cold nights in the winter months, we would give our boy a warm gruel or mash to get him through until morning. Oh, and some of those nights were not easy – rain, high winds, snowstorms, temperatures in the teens, blizzards. It never occurred to any of us to miss a feeding. It was all done out of love...

Some of you might be interested in what we fed our little guy. His staples, of course, were hay or orchard grass until he could not chew well. He loved his timothy hay, only if it was green and fresh. Sometimes we'd get an orchard grass and timothy mixture. From the start, we learned that giving a pony alfalfa was much too rich.

In the early years, the hay was supplemented with his sweet feed, the molasses and oats mixture. When we recognized that also was too rich for our boy, we moved to a balanced diet of Equine Senior pellets, later adding timothy or orchard grass pellets, all softened with hot water.

The job of going out for all Pony's supplies fell on my shoulders. One of my favorite places was a Tractor Supply in Flanders, N.J. I'll never forget the first few times walking into the store in full habit. It certainly wasn't the usual attire you find in a farming supply place. But

81

before long, we all greeted one another warmly by name, and still do. Thank you for all those years.

Hay was always a different story altogether. It was never easy to locate a reliable source of fresh timothy or orchard grass after Backers. Later in Pony's life when his teeth became an issue, we needed to find a source of hay that was easy to chew. We learned that Alpacas don't have teeth in the top front of their mouths, and need soft hay. We found a small Alpaca Farm within 15 minutes' drive from us. It was a treat to go over there and see the adorable Alpacas. I'd often take others with me so they too could have time with the sweet animals. We'd like to thank Nick and his family at Bluebird Farm Alpacas in Peapack.

Before we forget, one very important thing that shouldn't be left out, certainly for the pony… whatever season it was, our boy would get a carrot or an apple in the morning and late afternoon. He often would push the apple aside with his nose, and wait until he finished his meal, maybe occasionally taking a bite. Repeatedly he would do that, so we figured he was saving the best for last. Often at the nighttime feeding, as we approached with his pellets or warm mash, he would push his "bowl" towards us impatiently.

If we were a little late arriving in the evening, as we got close to his fence he'd give a soft nicker, as if he were saying, "what took you so long? I've been waiting…" And there were times when the nicker wasn't so soft, but a louder sustained guttural sound he'd make in his throat, as if complaining to us, "you're late."

When the pony first arrived on our property, he was wearing a halter. It appeared old, quite worn, and much too large for our boy. We guessed it might have been from the auction where he was purchased by the people down the road.

For some time, the vets were encouraging us to get our boy to wear a halter rather than trying to rope him, as it obviously would be easier for them to do their job. So, after picking up a halter that was closer to his size (it was a bright Kelly green) we decided to see what could be done.

Nine years after the pony came to us, Sr. Linda Clare entered community in 2001, coming with experience with horses. A few weeks before a vet was scheduled to visit, the two of us would go out every day to his area and work with him.

We used the "clicker method" which was an approach for training dogs and other animals that proved effective. Without going into detail, it is basically a variation of positive-reinforcement training using a small handheld device that makes a "clicking" sound. The clicker communicates the exact moment your dog (or pony!) does what you want. The timing is essential, and every click must be immediately followed by a reward. And as you already know, Pony loved to eat...

In 2005 the pony developed a serious infection in his left eye that we treated with antibiotics. The diagnosis led to the suggestion by a few vets to remove the eye as they said he would go blind. I was shocked, but trusted their opinion as they were professionals. They proposed to transport the pony up to Cornell for the procedure.

On the given day, several people showed up in the case they might be needed. A lead strap that ostensibly could hold a 2000 lb. horse was first hooked to his halter, then attached to a tree in his smaller enclosure. As the vet approached the pony with the syringe to sedate him, Pony jerked his neck up, the strap snapped, and he bolted. Although the group was circled around him, he saw an opening and ran directly toward it, heading to the back. That to me was a sign, and perhaps the one I was waiting for. I thanked everyone for coming, apologizing for any inconvenience it might have caused. I told the vets to cancel everything.

He did not allow a halter to be put on after that. You couldn't even get near him holding one in your hand.

There was no change in Pony's left eye in the years that followed, except that it had a milky appearance. We are sure he could see shadows.

He never went blind.

"...transcending linear time"

While writing this book and recalling the years Pony was with us, other incidents came to mind that clearly stand out, seemingly insignificant at the time they occurred. Yet in hindsight, these moments appear to take on an of their own, illumined, shining out like sparklers in the night.

Let me share a personal experience as an example, yet having completely been lost to my conscious awareness until now. Perhaps you may be able to relate something similar in your own life...

I was at a crossroads, about to embark on a journey into the unknown, having made the decision to enter the religious life. Dear Father Maitland was spending some time with me before the ceremony to be received as a novice, the first level toward becoming a nun. It was late May, and the weather was gorgeous... iridescent blue sky, not too hot.

We sat outside, behind the convent where it would be quiet, away from the comings and goings of the staff and sisters. It was rather awkward at first because I really wasn't quite sure of what to say. But my nervousness began to be assuaged due to Fr. Maitland's relaxed manner and sense of humor. He was a good listener.

After standing up from where we were, on the steps going down from the cloister, we slowly walked over toward one of the summer houses.

Once we entered, we sat across from each other, not speaking for quite a while, taking in the beauty of our surroundings. From my perspective I could see out across the beautiful green grass, lined by cedar trees.

The center of the grounds, with stairs leading down to the area, was once a Victorian English Garden, many years before. The pear and apple trees were in blossom, the fragrance almost intoxicating...

It was one of those special moments when time seems to shift into a different dimension, when everything feels suspended or held in place, transcending linear time as we know it...

It felt like an eternity before either of us spoke.

I smiled and said, "wouldn't this be a perfect setting for a horse?" imagining one out in the middle of the pasture.

A year later our beloved pony appeared, seemingly out of nowhere.

Just a coincidence you say?
Perhaps...

As mentioned earlier, the pony was living with us for 27 years, and we think he was about age 7 or 8 when he first showed up on our property. So that puts our boy at around 34 or 35 years old when the end came and he "crossed over." Although there is hesitation to share about the last days of his life, it will provide a sense of closure for all of us. Please know it is not easy to write, but it needs be written. It is all part of the miracle, the cycle of life and death.

In the late spring of 2019, we began to notice the pony would lie down a lot more than usual in the middle of the day. But we thought it was due to possible sore feet from eating too much grass. For several months he had some swelling on the side of his face that was treated with antibiotics. It would seem to disappear, but then return.

There was hesitation on my part to call the vet's office again. I had a strange premonition I could not shake, that if they came, he would have to be put down. It took several weeks before setting up an appointment.

One afternoon, Pony was standing by his fence. I approached him, and he looked at me as if he was trying to tell me something, with eye contact between us lasting for some time. I did not realize what it was about until hindsight.

Our boy left this earth a week later. The vet did come, Dr. Meghan Hayes from B.W. Furlong and Associates. Many images were taken with a portable x-ray machine, and the resulting prognosis was not good. It was a soft tissue mass growing in his upper jaw. In response to a later text message I sent questioning the prognosis, Dr. Hayes very graciously explained, "the disease process affecting his palate was advanced enough that he had a very poor prognosis to heal. Taking quality of life into consideration is where my recommendation to lay him to rest came from. He was struggling to breathe through his one nostril and had extremely pale gums." And she continued, saying, "I know how big of a loss this is for you and my heart breaks for you."

The end came very quickly. The pony just took a long deep sigh, and that was it.

I could not leave him. I wanted to be there alongside him to see him off on his next journey.

With a finger or two, I gently traced around the contours of his face and nose, talking and singing softly to him. It is said that when someone or any living creature takes their last breath, the auditory sense is the last to go.

I am sure he heard my voice… our sweet boy.

…where the pony took his last breath.

Several months passed, and we thought there should be some kind of memorial service for our boy. So, on St. Francis day October 4, when we usually have an informal outdoor Blessing of the animals, we remembered the pony. Dr. Marne Platt, one of Pony's first vets if you recall, offered to give us something for our loss, a donation toward whatever we considered to be appropriate.

We had a river rock engraved, placing it on the grass where he took his last breath.

In loving memory
"PONY"
June 11, 2019

A number of people attended the little service, some bringing their four-legged friends for a blessing. It was a beautiful day, not unlike the day in June when the pony moved on to the next life.

A printed program was given to all those who came, including an insert for Pony. Sr. Barbara Jean put the booklet together and presided over the service. Those present participated in the responses.

The program in color:

Blessing of the Animals

for

St. Francis Day

Oct 4, 2019

Here is the insert for the pony:

Remembering Pony

We thank you our God, for all of the many animals in our world, both tame and wild. Especially we thank you for Pony, who adopted us to be his family.

Thank you for his long life and his healing presence, especially for our guests, who came to visit him.

Thank you also for St. Francis, who preached to the birds and befriended the animals. May we follow his example. In Jesus' Name we pray - *Amen.*

In a larger format:

Remembering Pony

We thank you our God, for all the many animals in our world, both tame and wild. Especially we thank you for Pony, who adopted us to be his family.

Thank you for his long life and his healing presence, especially for our guests, who came to visit him.

Thank you also for St. Francis, who preached to the birds and befriended the animals. May we follow his example. In Jesus' Name we pray – *Amen.*

The little service booklet continues on the following page:

For the good earth which God has given us, and for the wisdom and will to conserve it, and for peace, health, happiness, justice, and good will among all its creatures, let us pray to the Lord.
Lord, have mercy.

For God's mercy and protection upon all animals, and especially those that are injured or abused, hungry or deserted, lost or dying, let us pray to the Lord.
Lord, have mercy.

For grateful hearts and gentle hands and for a spirit of respect and wonder for the animals entrusted to our care, let us pray to the Lord.
Lord, have mercy.

For God's blessing on the animals who give us their loyal companionship and continually remind us of God's unconditional love for us and all creation, let us pray to the Lord.
Lord, have mercy.

Blessed are you, our God, eternal King, for making every creature that lives in earth and sea and sky. Blessed are you for your servant Francis who called them all his brothers and sisters. By the power of thy love, enable every creature to live according to your plan. May all your works forever praise you, O Father, Son, and Holy Spirit.
Amen.

Blessing of the Animals
[Name], We ask God's blessing on you in the Name of the Holy and Undivided Trinity who made us all. May you be healthy and live in harmony with all God's creatures.
Amen.

When the pony came to us, never could we possibly know what the future would bring and how this little guy would change all our lives. Was it just by chance that he showed up on our property, seemingly appearing out of nowhere?

Or was something else at work, a power or energy greater than us. Call it what you will - the Creator, Universal Life force, the Great Spirit, God...

It's almost as if this little horse - this mystical, magical being - was placed here, remaining in our lives for a time. And then was just taken from us, only to be returned to whence he came.

On a soft summer's evening, if you are standing by the pony's fence, you can feel his presence.

He's still with us, in spirit...

PONY'S POINT OF VIEW

The community newsletter was a way of connecting with our friends, associates, school alumnae and oblates. It had news of the sisters, and went out 3 times during the year. Each of our four-legged companions living with us wrote a column, with photos included. So many people over the years said they loved reading the animal stories and looked forward to them whenever the newsletter came out.

We thought you'd like to read "PONY'S POINT OF VIEW," but in a different format. Rather than seeing them appear every few months, the pony columns will be printed here, one after the other. You might think of each entry as a personal letter, giving you a glimpse into the pony's reality and how he perceives his surroundings. You will see the seasons change, through his eyes, and how he appreciates nature.

Set free your imagination and release the child within you, and perhaps a smile will come to your face...

Spring 1993

Hello everyone. I'm not sure if we've met. Did you know that the sisters have given me a forever home? I'll be writing a column in their newsletter from now on. I hope you'll like reading it.

Well, it looks like warmer days are finally here. Thank God! That cold white stuff was getting on my nerves. And the wind! But I always found the warm sheltered places in the back, occasionally staying in the shed the sisters' friends built for me (just so their feelings wouldn't be hurt.) They also put up more fencing to let everyone know the back forte was my territory - especially the hunters.

It was really nice to have fresh water at room temperature during those cold spells, being kept from freezing by a heating element. I didn't mind if my friends drank from the bucket either (the cat, dog, squirrels, deer and birds.)

I really am grateful for this new life, even though I may not show my appreciation much. After all, you do realize I have to keep up this image they have of me and look wild-eyed and unmanageable just so they don't get any ideas of taming me. Basically, I am still free, and I always will be…

October 1993

I have a few moments to write this, and then I have to get back to my favorite pastime. Not too many days left of good grazing, you know…

It's been a year since my arrival to the Community. The fenced enclosures have proven to be quite adequate, yet occasionally I feel twinges of missing the open spaces. But I guess life is often a series of trade-offs, isn't it? Every morning and late afternoon I know that wonderful molasses sweet feed will be there for me (as well as those apples falling from the trees!) No complaints here. The sisters have been good to me…

Last week while eating my molasses oats later in the day, I could hear voices coming from the sitting room above me. The Sisters and friends were singing some song that had my name in it and the word 'birthday." A few moments later one of them appeared carrying a small cake that had the shape of a carrot in the icing and a few little flames on top. And I got a piece of it! Oh, that was so sweet, so delicious…

Not much more to say, except that I'm content and I have relative peace of mind. So, I guess I'll return to my grazing. Very contemplative, very contemplative…

Winter 1993

The leaves are off the trees, no more apples on the ground, and no grass for grazing… and all I seem to be doing is standing around. Sometimes that silly cat comes tearing across the yard right in front of me. I cannot understand that kind of behavior - it just doesn't make any sense to me.

The old dog (Pucker) occasionally walks back here, but isn't too interested in getting to know me (not too surprising, considering I stay pretty much to myself, minding my own business.) And once in a while, one of those two-legged creatures walks through my territory, carrying a book in her hands. How can she do that? Walk and look at a book simultaneously?!! (I think her name is Sr Barbara Jean.)

Admittedly, the hay and sweet feed are the highlights of my day. Otherwise, my time is spent these days watching, and waiting. They tell me that's what Advent is all about. Hmm…

(Please notice my "whiskers" and thick winter coat!)

I hope your Christmas is filled with Blessings.

Spring 1994

At last, the earth is finally peeking out from under the snow, and I just cannot resist the opportunity to roll in the mud…

it feels so good, especially now that my winter coat is beginning to loosen and fall off. I usually wait until the weekend to get into the rolling, when a lot of people are around. I must admit I do a bang-up job, covered from nose to tail with mud! They all just don't understand how wonderful it is, the smell of the earth, and the cool wetness on my back. I guess humans will be humans…

(I still had that ungodly halter that was put on at the auction.)

The winter was a little rough. But back here there are lots of protected spots available to get out of the wind and freezing rain. Actually, I don't mind being out during a snowfall, especially one of those quiet ones. There's nothing like standing out here during the night, motionless, when the snow is falling - everything is so still, so very still…

Spring will bring the flowers, and the grass! Oh, just the thought of green grass sends me into a peaceful reverie. Before long I can resume my grazing, the grazing I so dearly love to do.

101

Fall 1994

Well, this was certainly an autumn to remember for some time! The apple trees behind the convent and the pear trees in my back enclosure were just heavy with fruit. It was a bumper crop this year, to be sure. I'm guessing that all the snow we had this past winter had something to do with it. The sisters were concerned that I might get sick if I ate all that fruit, so they closed off the back orchard (the apple trees.)

But the pear trees are in my back enclosure, so they tried roping the area off. And all I had to do was put my head under the rope (they should give me a little more credit... I do have a brain.) So, what did they come up with next? They tied a brick on the end of a long rope, then tossed it as high as they could. Once wrapped around a branch they began pulling, repeatedly. As I stood there watching from a distance, one pear after another came thumping to the ground. Then the wheel barrels were brought in, and after filling them with the pears they were rolled out from my area. One after another (oh the frustration!)

But I guess I just have to be appreciative for what I have.

I am certainly enjoying the cooler weather. I hope you are too. Have a wonderful fall.

December 1994

I guess it's that time again, being expected to say something for the newsletter. Folks don't realize there's not much to report when one lives this life of leisure. Until recently, the grazing's been great. But now the leaves are all off the trees, so no more grass. Good hay, though, and more of it than grass! And of course, those delicious molasses oats make my day.

So, you probably wonder, what do I do with all my time? I just hang out, attentively listening to what's going on around me. Sometimes I get a little nervous because of rustling in the leaves nearby, only to find it's just a squirrel or some Starlings. A turkey wandered into my territory the other day and couldn't figure how to get out. Silly bird.

I do miss the pears and the apples. I just don't understand why my two-legged human friends kept hauling them out. Anyway, as I said before, there is much to be grateful for...

(...a special moment with Sr Margo)

A blessed Christmas to you all.

Easter 1995

The winter was really quite nice, only one snowstorm as I recall and not terribly cold. As you already know, I don't mind brisk weather as long as it isn't freezing rain. And there are my favorite places where I can find shelter from the elements.

Please note the new overhang extension built on the back of my shed last year.

At last tiny sprouts of green are making their way up through the dry dead grass left from before the winter. Certainly not enough to satisfy this appetite, but a foretaste of what's to come!

Have a wonderful spring! I hope you enjoy it, as I will…

October 1995

I thought it was time for another one of those newsletters. It's getting colder, my winter coat is already beginning to grow, and the apples are falling! I just can't understand why there aren't any pears this year.

This weather is great. No more flies that really drive me crazy. Yet on the hot afternoons I could lose them by going into my shed, or rolling on the dusty ground. And there's a lot of shade back here, and trees that smell good (I think they are called Cedars.)

(when I was still loose on the school grounds. The cottage is next to the school.)

It was this time of year when I began living with the sisters, in the autumn. I believe it's been three years now.

I am truly grateful.

1995 Winter (Christmas)

Well, when "first light" illuminated enough of my living space this morning, I could see that everything was covered with white. As you know, I really like the snow, as long as there is no wind.

And of course, the one disappointing part of winter is that grazing is of the question. Although there are always the bushes in back of the convent, you know, that wonderful Hedgerow that surrounds the orchard?

Great for snacking…

But don't worry, I get plenty of hay!

Oh, before I forget, I want to wish you all a wonderful Christmas and Winter, filled with the blessings of joy, smiles and laughter.

Love,
pOnY

Spring 1996
Needless to say, it was certainly a winter we all will not forget! That white stuff really isn't an issue for me, but when it comes in quantities of thirty inches or more at a time, it is something to contend with. But the days are growing longer, and Spring is coming, gradually…

The grazing is not much to write home about, yet if one goes through the motions perhaps the grass will appear sooner? So, I am already out there nibbling away, giving the impression that the grass is rich and green, and succulent…

Oh, I might add one note of sadness. Pucker, the sisters' old dog, is gone (I love this photo with snow on her nose.)

She was a good friend. I will miss her.
A Blessed Easter to you all.

107

October 1996

Hello to everyone! Hope you had a good summer. Mine was rather uneventful, but for the usual annoyances of flies and the sisters trying to spray me with some kind of perfumey stuff they call Avon Skin So Soft. What do they think I am? A sissy? Anyway, if I go into my shed the flies don't bug me so much... (bug me, get it?) The shed smells so good in there (I think it's pine.) So much more appropriate for an outdoorsman, don't you think?

I might as well mention the new family member. His name is Petie. The Sisters found him at St Hubert's Giralda. He's one and a half years old, almost, and he is sometimes a royal pain because he always wants to run and play with me. Occasionally is understandable, but when it's hot or while I'm grazing?

Nevertheless, it's nice to have company, especially in the morning when they put him out on the run. Then he's fairly civilized and we touch noses and have a good chat.

Enjoy your autumn.

"pOnY"

Christmas 1996

As you already know, there's another addition to our small community... the dog. He's OK, I guess. But when he gets loose and comes back here to my territory while I'm grazing, interrupting my meditation, I do not appreciate it. He just doesn't understand, when I'm grazing, I do not want to be disturbed. The sisters know that, and respect my need for space.

I have to admit though, we do occasionally have a good romp together. We take turns chasing each other. Petie is very fast!

It's the time of year again when anticipation is in the air, a kind of waiting for something very special. I can sense it. It's usually quiet back here, and it feels good just to stand in the warm sun, listening and looking around...

I hope you have a wonderful Advent, Christmas and Epiphany. Such a wonderful season of the year. Yes, it is a season. Christmas is not just one day!

As Always,
pOnY

Spring 1997

Thank God, winter is over and behind us. But it wasn't
nearly as bad as last year. January '96 was brutal! We had
that blizzard early in the month, with 30 inches of snow.
Actually, it was quite exciting! I usually like to stand under
my overhang and wait out the storm. And in the morning
Ryan came out and shoveled a path from my shed to the
fence. I was well taken care of, as always…

Can you believe it is already past the middle of March?
I always know because the little white flowers along the
cloister wall are the first to come up, and the birds are
singing more. The tiny blades of new grass are inching their
way through the decayed leaves, which as you probably can
guess, gives me great joy!

Let's welcome spring with hearts filled with awe…

Fall 1997

Finally, autumn is here! I thought it never would arrive. Yet the months have gone by rather quickly, don't you think? The last time we connected was in the spring, in March, I believe.

The apples this year are not as abundant as they were last fall, following that huge snowstorm in early January. Do you remember a few winters ago when we had all that snow and there were so many apples and pears the following autumn? Do you think it might be a pattern?

Anyway, they've closed off the apple orchard, again, so I can't get to the apples. But what I find most interesting is that the pear tree in the back enclosure, you know, the one with all those pears a few years ago, has not had any more since then. It's like the tree just needed a rest! Hm. I find that rather curious, don't you? We can learn from nature...

(I guess Sr Margo felt sorry for me and gave me an apple...)

I hope you have a good autumn. Try to take some time to really experience all that comes with the changing rhythm of the seasons. Carve a pumpkin, eat a candied apple, go for a hike in the woods...

Christmas 1997

Well, once again the leaves have all fallen off the trees, and the weather is getting colder. The ground is hard under foot now, not the soft earth which I love so much. And of course, not much grass left to graze. There's always that wonderful herb garden someone planted in *my* territory, so occasionally I enjoy a tasty snack in between meals.

Unfortunately, I haven't seen any more of those red, round, sweet apples... they are gone by late autumn. It's kind of fun to just stand there in the back orchard on a windy day, just listening for the thump where it hits the ground. I walk over to it ever so casually (so it doesn't look like I am too excited about it, of course.) Ah, I then take small bites, making it last as long as possible. I really try to get every one of those delicious treats that lands in my habitat.

But one thing that perplexes me... my personal physician thinks I should lose some weight. I really don't understand that. What do you think? It's really my thick winter coat. Really…

Have a blessed Advent and Christmastide.
Enjoy your winter.

Spring 1998

Hi, everyone. Seems like a long time again since writing to you. Can you believe it is already spring? I don't know about you, but I am still anticipating winter to really set in. It never came! I even grew a thick coat for the cold... (well, to be honest, I cannot take the credit for *that.*)

But last night we had a lovely snowfall, the kind that starts slowly, almost imperceptibly... landing so gently on the ground and on the branches of the trees. There is something almost holy about it.

I am not so sure if Petie notices how lovely the snow is. He gets a little crazy and likes to run around in circles, and even bites at the white stuff. He's still kind of immature, I guess. Oh well. I just ignore him when he acts up...

Before I forget, I hope you all have a wonderful Easter and spring! Let us celebrate Resurrection, yes, with every new blade of grass and flower that springs up from the earth...

It's so great to be alive, isn't it?

Love,
pOnY

Fall 1998

At last, the cooler weather has returned, and I can feel my winter coat growing already. On some of those warm days, it is not very comfortable, believe me! But no complaints... The summer was really not that bad, for me anyway. There are so many refreshingly cool places back here in my territory where I can just "hang out" as they say.

And yet, it always seems just when I begin drifting off into an afternoon siesta, I can hear the jingle of Petie's collar, and I know I'm in for a chase (although the sisters seem to know not to let him out on those beastly hot days... thank God!) If he would only learn I am usually willing to give him a good run for his money, but it's the "in your face" barking that is so annoying. Why can't he have fun without that incessant noise?! I won't give up on him, though. As I often say, just give him a little more time and he'll grow up.

The autumn days are ahead, the pure light, the crisp nights, the brilliant colors... and the trees releasing their leaves. It is a time of letting go, isn't it? Everything is different when we take the opportunity to reflect on the rhythm of the seasons, and possibly learn from the changes and transformation in the air...

Take care of yourselves. Carpe diem.

Christmas 1998
Greetings dear friends! Although it's only been a few months since our last newsletter, it's always good to connect with you.

The excitement before Christmas is clearly felt by children and adults alike (as well as us four-legged creatures!) There is almost a magical feeling in the air, especially for kids. I'm sure most of you remember awakening Christmas morning, wondering, did Santa come? Did he bring what you asked for?

When we are older, for many of us it is quite different. The importance of gifts is replaced with the birth of a little Child, and the presents become something else...

Presence.

Easter/Spring 1999

Hello everyone! Well, it really looks as if spring is finally on its way at last, doesn't it? The snowdrops are up everywhere in the area where I hang out. And the daffodils are poking their heads through the earth. The ground isn't so hard to walk on anymore, and feels cushiony under my feet. And from just after dawn to mid-morning the birds are really creating an awful racket! But I don't mind. It's just another sign, a sign of new life, new beginnings... new life bursting forth from the dark confines of the earth, reaching toward the sun....
(I bet you didn't think I could be that deep, did you? Don't forget, I spend hours back here with lots of time to ponder and contemplate the important things like God and nature.)

Michaelmas 1999

Once again, it's the time of year when the colorful leaves are being released, the temperature is cooler at night, and the days are getting shorter. I don't know about you, but I really love the autumn. But part of me gets a little depressed because it gets darker so soon. I miss the long days of summer (but can do without the heat and humidity!)

Yet the quality of light in the fall is so different. I spend hours just watching the sun and the shadows. There is something special about the daylight in late September and October. Have you ever noticed?

The presence of God is everywhere, here, now, at any given moment… Indulge.

Spring 2000

Isn't it wonderful? The grass is getting green once more, the flowers are coming up… and the days are longer! The earth is now soft under foot and the fragrance of the air is almost intoxicating. Have you heard the birds singing? I am already awake at dawn (not a heavy sleeper…) I know some of the sisters are complaining that the birds are so loud they are waking them up. It's good for them (the sisters.) Brings them closer to nature, closer to the earth… sometimes I wonder what they do all day long. Why don't I see them out here enjoying God's Creation? They seem to be always so busy. I know whatever they do is important, like praying and all that. But there is nothing like being out here in the quiet of the night in a full moon, or in the early hours of the morning.

The presence of the Divine is so very real at night and in the early morning. I am just so filled with awe and gratitude at moments like these. I just wish someone was out here with me to share these experiences.

Oh, well.

And before I forget, have a wonderful Easter and Spring. Take in the new life all around you…

Fall 2000

Greetings, everyone... please forgive me if I say this every year! Ah, yes, the cooler weather is here. I don't know about you, but for those of you who also live in this state, New Jersey summers can often be, well, how can I put this, not very comfortable, to say the least. I've heard the humidity is worse here than in Florida! And when one lives outside (as does a guy like myself) one has to contend with all that goes with that. The small flies are not too bad, but the horse flies are the bane of my existence. They drive me crazy (even when I get sprayed with that sweet stuff.) I can be grazing contentedly and one of those buggers bites me on my back - a place I cannot possibly get to even if I try. I am sure the sisters have seen me when I race in from the large pasture area and head into my shed! For some reason they don't seem to come in there (the horseflies, that is.) Thank God!

So, what plans do you have for the Fall? I've heard that a lot of people take vacation time in September or October. A wonderful time of year to travel. Sometimes I dream of far off places and try to imagine what it would be like.
But please don't get me wrong. I love it here.

Winter 2000

It was the evening after that first big snow. There was a beautiful full moon, and everything was just soaked in a milky white luminescence. I was just meandering along in the back part of my enclosure and happened to notice a break in the fence. Hmm, I thought, maybe there's some decent grass out near the cemetery.

So, out I went, and began pawing at the snow with my hoof to get at the grass.

I don't know how long I was out there - when I am grazing there's kind of a time warp. And here comes Sr Margo, calling to me and wanting me to follow her. She had that container in her hand and I could hear food in it. OK. I'll follow her. But whenever I got close enough and almost into the container, she kept gently pulling it away, holding it just beyond my reach. Suddenly we were by the cars parked near the garage, and a wall of plowed snow was right in front of me. I felt closed in, and turned and ran to the front yard. Ah, yes... the grass was green and succulent. I am not budging, I thought. And I didn't. I continued pawing at the snow and eating that delicious cold grass, totally oblivious to my surroundings. Heaven.

I had no idea how long I'd been out there. In the wee hours of the morning my grazing was disrupted with some noise from the woods nearby. Looking around, I became very disoriented. I could see the convent, that familiar white building, but it looked different (I was in the front of it, not behind as I usually am.)

Just before dawn, I heard that familiar voice again. This time I was ready, as I had been out for the entire night. I followed her back into the enclosure where there were some cut up apples mixed in with my feed, and a large portion of hay awaiting me. Thank God!

A few days have gone by, and it all seemed like a dream. I really love my life just the way it is... and I hope you all feel the same about yours.

My wish for you this Advent season is that it is filled with blessings.

I hope Christmas will be meaningful and, yes, Holy. May the little Christ child be born anew for each of us.

Spring 2001

Greetings everyone. I would dearly love to say Happy Spring to you all, yet what really gets in the way of doing so is my hesitation due to the yearly arrival of the dreaded little "no-see-ums." (Gnats.) But let me tell you a funny story that Sr. Margo once shared with me (we do talk often.) The first time she led a group to Ireland, the hotel where they stayed at the beginning of the trip was in a lovely setting in the heart of the Wicklow Mountains called Glendalough. When she went to open a window, as she always does, she noticed a little sign on the windowsill. It read, MIND THE MIDGIES. She hadn't a clue what midgies were, but she knew the Irish had a great sense of humor and wondered if "midgies" was just another word for the "little people." She learned the next day that midgies were those tiny gnats. (You can smile now.)

Anyway, putting aside my obvious dislike for the tiny bugs, I do enjoy all the new life around me. I love to look for the snowdrops, the crocuses and the daffodils, knowing I will find them in

the same places as before. But the tiny sweet white flowers in the recesses of the stone wall, you know, near the Flemish Cross, are my favorite.

But as you know, the activity I love the most is grazing... Have a great Spring.

Fall 2001

Well, this is not going to be an easy column to write for the newsletter, but I need to say a few words...

Earlier in the autumn there was a day that will not ever be forgotten. It was beautiful and mild, with the kind of blue sky that I love. Yet there was something strange about that particular morning...

I was out by my fence, and noticed how quiet it was. It was almost eerie. I sensed something was not right but could not understand what it was. I could hear sisters' voices coming from the refectory. The TV was on, and I thought that was strange, as breakfasts are usually in silence. Why would the TV be turned on? The news announcer was loud, speaking in a very excited voice. What was going on?

(*editor's note:* As you all can already guess, the date was Sept 11, 2001. Everyone will remember exactly where they were on that terrible morning. When first walking into the room where the TV was on, it did not seem possible that it was actually happening. Was it some strange science fiction movie? It felt so surreal...) Let's pray something like this will never happen again.

Winter 2001

Hello, everyone.

There is something special about trees in winter, their silhouettes creating lace-like patterns against the backdrop of the sky. Trees become their essential nature without their leaves, or with maybe a few dry ones left on the branches. The sound of the wind is different, too, when there aren't any leaves on the trees. And the daylight during the winter months… so pure, so clean.

I get more reflective in winter. I really don't have much choice in the matter... my usual routine of grazing is brought to a close. So, there's lots of time for pondering, and for just being still. I highly recommend it.

May I wish you blessings of this lovely season. Y' know, hanging out here in my enclosure behind the convent can be an experience that would be worthwhile for all of you. As you know, I do a lot of watching, and listening. It is usually so quiet. Time seems to stand still.

Take care of yourselves. Life is precious.

Spring 2002

It's been 10 years now since I found the sisters and have lived in the back enclosure. The snow fencing they put up was only going to be "temporary." I guess they figured I wouldn't be around so long! I hate to tell them, but guys like me often live to well over 35 years. I think I am about 15 now, so if my health stays good the sisters will still be taking care of me well into their 70's. Poor dears, I can just see them toddling out here to scoop you know what… they must really love me to put up with it all, and believe me there is a lot of it!

Spring is here… isn't it marvelous? Each morning I love to stand and watch the sun come up over the trees and listen to the birds. It's fun to try to pick out which bird is the first to start chirping in the morning. I think it's usually the robin. As I've said before, everyone is just so busy these days. God must get a little sad, because people just don't seem to find the time to spend with Him anymore, out in nature… they always seem to have more important things to be doing. Hmmm… when you think about it, what really is more important than seeking the Presence of God?

Try to take some quiet for yourselves… get up early and listen to the birds! And have a Blessed Easter.

September 2002

At last, the cooler weather has returned. I can feel my winter coat already growing. The summer was quite hot with little rain, but there are so many cool places back here in my territory where I can just "hang out" as they say.

Some sad news. My little friend Patches is gone. She has not been out to visit me for a long time, and I saw them carry her out a few weeks ago. I knew she would not be back. She used to sit on the fence post or come and rub against my legs.

Sometimes we just were quiet together, something like what the sisters call praying.

I believe she is now in a good place, but I will miss her.

Winter 2002

Ah, yes… there is nothing like a winter's day with snow on the ground, an iridescent blue sky, and the light from the sun so pure and sparkling. I love a day like that, don't you? Even the trees take on a different appearance in the winter, like sentinels guarding the earth. Yet there is something very vulnerable about trees without their leaves, isn't there? Open and exposed to the elements of wind and ice, trees withstand quite a battering.

Winter should be a season for slowing down, a time for reflection, and for possibly going inward. Just as the trees are dormant in the winter, and the life force suspended until spring, we too might rest. If we could only learn from nature…

I wish for you a season filled with blessings, and perhaps a time of holiness. Take a moment here and there to pause and linger in wonderment and awe of God's wonderful Creation.

And if you have the time to spare, maybe say a few prayers for all those who are struggling for their lives, for those who are alone, for teenagers on the streets…

Ah, Spring! You could never guess from this photo though.
I still have my winter whiskers and snow is on the ground.
Have you noticed how loud the birds are chattering? And
they appear to be so busy. No more snow and ice… the
ground under my feet is not hard anymore, the earth gives a
little as I walk all around back here in my enclosure. The
grass is beginning to come up, so tender and succulent… the
air is different, too… sweeter, more fragrant. Such peace. It
seems that everywhere else it would be the same… but
somehow, I know it isn't.

There are nights when I am out here alone, and I see awful
visions of explosions, and the sky is red. Somewhere in the
world there are terrible things going on… is it a dream or a
nightmare?

One morning we may awaken to a new dawn, and it will all
be over. The world can begin anew, re-building trust and
respect among all its creatures. Let's pray it is soon.

Fall 2003

Hello friends!

Well, the nights are getting cooler, have you noticed? Oh, and the crickets are soooo loud! I think they're called katy-dids. Where did they ever get that name? I always know when summer is almost over when I hear them, and autumn is just around the corner. I certainly don't mind as the flies do get to me as you know. Ah, I love the fall, shuffling through the dry leaves, seeing the vapor of your breath, feeling so alive...

(I thought this might be a good photo for a portrait. What do you think?)

Hope you all are well.

Take care of yourselves... life is precious.

Christmas 2003

So here we are again approaching the Christmas season and 'rounding the yearly cycle. Advent is often considered to be the beginning of the liturgical Church calendar. Surprised I know that? Don't forget, I've been here since 1992 so it's impossible that some of this doesn't rub off on me. But my own frame of reference does not revolve around the Church calendar! Just to remind you all, I live outdoors all the time. So, the weather is my primary reality…

Looking back over this past year, we had w e a t h e r. All I can remember about last winter from February on was cold and snow. I hoped we would get a break once December arrived this year. But, alas, no such luck. We had two big snowstorms in the first few weeks of December. Enough already!

Well, we can only hope the remainder of the winter will be more forgiving than this past one.

A Blessed holiday season to you all.

Take time for delighting in the miracle of life. It comes 'round only once.

130

Spring 2004

And here we are again! Spring is just around the corner, as they say. At first glance it still appears to be winter, but if you really look closely there are the signs of new life everywhere.

Out in our woods there are of course the snowdrops pushing through the dead decayed leaves... and along the south side of the convent where it is warm and sunny, you can see little green shoots coming up along the foundation of the house.

And the birds are noisy, seemingly very busy...

Yup, signs of new life, new beginnings... Once again, I've said it before and I'll say it again, it's great to be alive!

Hope each of you can take some time to watch and listen to the changes that are taking place. So much is happening that we cannot see, in the earth, in the trees, in the plants.
It's all a mystery to me...

131

Fall 2004

It's time once again for a newsletter! I get the feeling you all have heard so much of this before. I don't want to bore you with repetition. Yet, living out back here can be, well, rather routine. You know, just hanging out, day after day. But, on the other hand, one can learn a lot from living simply. I have everything I need, really… shelter from the wind and rain; plenty of grass, as well an apple here and there from the apple trees; fresh water and hay; and protection from the flies (they spray me twice a day in the hot weather.)

So, when all my needs are met, I can spend more time contemplating God's creation! I love watching for the sunrise, as you already know. I try to stand in just the right spot for that breaking of a new day. Oh, and listening for the first bird to wake up. Could be a Robin, or maybe a Carolina Wren… and of course, just around sunset from May through July one can almost be transported by the sound of the Thrush. I just love the Thrush's song, don't you? So very quieting…

I hope you all had a wonderful summer. Here we are at the beginning of September already. Can you believe it?

Enjoy your Autumn.

Winter 2004

Greetings to you all this very blustery December day! I hope your autumn was filled with blessings, as was mine. Admittedly, the fall harvest is always bountiful for me back here in my area, considering there are a few apple trees that are still bearing some fruit. Not too many apples, though. The sisters make sure of that! But they don't realize when the leaves drop off the trees they are also quite tasty. It's really kind of funny because when people see me they assume my rather rotund shape is because I am being fed too much... oh well. No one understands that it's very important to have some fat on you for the winter!   :o)

Furthermore, as I've said before, my winter coat is 2 inches thick, so that gives the impression that I am eating too much Why doesn't anyone believe me? Gosh, no one trusts me... Next time you visit I just might allow you to run your hand along my neck and shoulder and you will understand what I have been trying to tell you all these years.
I guess I am sounding a bit defensive. Sorry.

May your Christmas and New Year be filled with the blessings of peace, joy and love. And have a lovely winter. Catch up on some reading, do some quiet creative things like knitting or painting.

Spring 2005

Is winter truly over and gone? I certainly hope so… the signs
are everywhere, aren't they? It's warmer, the fragrance of
the air is so sweet, and the birds are just chortling away. The
sky brightens much earlier, and the daylight lasts into the
evening. Ah, Spring…

I was standing out in my back enclosure the other day, just
being attentive. It was very still, and I could just feel the
Presence of something very Holy. I live for those moments,
don't you? The cold winter nights - the wind, the snow and
ice - are mere memories now, already fading.

There was a joyful memory from years ago that came back
to me. It was when Petie and I were running together out
back. Oh, it was wonderful. We'd be just flying alongside
each other with such abandon, laughing all the way. It's
been years since we did that, yet the memory still lingers.
It's those kinds of thoughts that can really sustain us. I'm
sure you know what I mean…

I sincerely hope you had a very special Easter. It is only the
beginning of what the sisters call Eastertide, an entire season
that is full of new life all around us.

Fall 2005

Hi everyone! Once again, the nights are getting cooler and the Katy-dids are almost thunderous! And would you believe my winter coat is already beginning to grow.

A few of the sisters were standing near me just the other evening (they were getting all the burrs out of my mane and forelock). One of them noticed that my coat was getting thicker, and remarked about it, amazed because it hasn't been *that* cold. Well, did you know it doesn't have to do with colder temperatures, but with the days getting shorter? Yup. A horse's coat is like the leaves changing colors! Like photo something... is it photosynthesis? I think that's the word. Hmmm... but I didn't think I had any chlorophyll in my system. Hey, but I *do* eat a lot of grass. Think that has anything to do with it? I wonder...

Anyway, enjoy the days ahead as summer gently exits stage right or left, and autumn quietly moves in. As I've said often before, yes, it's all a miracle to me. We can learn so much from nature. Change, transition, transformation... and it happens so gradually.
Enjoy the days ahead.
Carpe diem.

Winter 2005

And now we move into Advent once more, offering the opportunity to just slow down. Spend some time outdoors, perhaps going for some walks in the woods, shuffling through the leaves.

Do you ever have the feeling you just can't give anymore? Yet if you take some quiet time each day, you'll be giving from an overflowing cup, rather than a cup that's almost empty.

Abundance, not scarcity...

"Give, and it will be given to you: good measure, pressed down, shaken together, and running over, will be given to you."

I hope you have a meaningful Advent. And on Christmas morning, let's all welcome the newborn Christ-child once again into our hearts... and remember the "reason for the season."

Spring 2006

Hello everyone.

Before I forget, although I hesitate somewhat, I want to say something about what's been going on now for several months. I developed an eye condition that might lead to blindness. They were going to remove my eye. The vets suggested driving me up to Cornell in Ithaca, NY, in a trailer. A lot of people came, but as soon as I realized the vet was about to tranquilize me with an injection, I snapped the lead and wouldn't let them get near me. I am not leaving my beloved enclosure! This is where I belong, and this is where I am going to stay. They'll have to come here to my own turf if they are considering any kind of treatment!

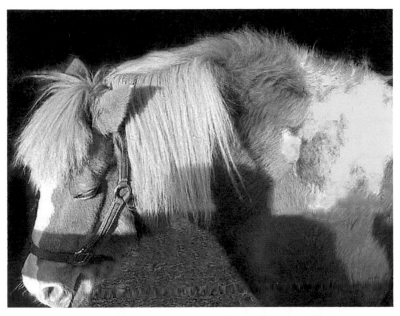

*(**please take note**: My sisters started working with me using a Clicker to train me to wear a halter. I trusted them, but then I could see there was a motive to it all. After this experience with the vets, I would never wear a halter again. Period. End of story.)*

OK, enough talking about me… let's get back to Spring.

I encourage you all to take the time, as I usually do, to stop and smell the flowers. Celebrate life!

Fall 2006

Greetings! It certainly looks like we all made it through another summer, didn't we? It wasn't too bad... the flies sometimes got to me, but I was able to get some relief from them by going into my shed. And it was cooler in there on those hot days in July!

I hope you don't mind, but there are a few new friends I'd like to introduce to you. I haven't had the pleasure of meeting them, but have heard so much about them. I am sure most of you are aware of our sisters in England? Well, they have a few four-legged residents in their life, just as the community does here in America. Let me introduce them to you:

This is Tabitha. She is quite shy. But if you look hard enough you might find her on a chair under the library table.

And this is Benedict. He often is found in the 'out' basket for mail in the library!

(Fall 2006 continued...)

Murphy belongs to Yvonne.
He is a character as you can see!

Do you happen to notice something quite remarkable? Don't you find there's a similarity with our Pete and Jack? Indeed! We just need to find a Tabitha (yet she does resemble our sweet Frideswide from years ago.) And to equal things out, our dear sisters across the Great Pond must consider, yes, a handsome horse like yours truly! (OK, pony...)

Enjoy each day to its fullest. Remember, life is precious...

Winter 2006

Hello, everyone… so good to be writing to you again. I must admit, it often feels a little strange, like talking into space… (not too much different sometimes when we pray, huh? We don't usually get a response! Maybe a subtle sign, or sensing something. Oh well.)

Nature is wonderful, isn't it? There is something very comforting about the changing of the seasons. Each time there's a familiarity, something known, yet it's still a miracle. Spring with its fresh yellow green leaves, iridescent against the blue sky. And fall when the leaves on the trees turn bright reds, oranges, yellow and gold. It's almost too much to bear sometimes. And then watching how the branches let go of their brilliant foliage, until one day only the silhouettes remain, like lace etched against the sky…

Winter is at last here. I am looking forward to the first snowfall, but not the ice, thank you very much. My coat is thick, and the soft earth is now hard, except out under the cedars where it remains cushiony under my feet.

I wish you a Blessed Advent and Nativity, filled with many moments of peace. Yes, again the familiarity, not unlike the seasons. And yes, once more the miracle…

Spring 2007

Hmmm... when was the last time we had a visit? It must have been around Christmas. The winter was rather forgiving, although we did have one cold spell, didn't we? As I've mentioned to you over the years, cold doesn't bother me that much, because after all, I have my thick winter coat that keeps me very warm. And I'm sure I've mentioned it before, the freezing rain is what really gets to me, although the shed is there for shelter. Oh, the wind makes me a little jittery, that fitful kind.

It's that time of year again when there is transformation everywhere... the hardened ground becomes soft once more, the grass turns green and begins to grow, the flowers sprout up through the dead leaves. The morning sun appears earlier, and sinks later and later each day. Birds are chattering, so busy building their nests. The seasonal cycle returns... new life, new beginnings.

I want to wish you a Blessed Eastertide. Jesus was supposed to have still been around for 40 days after the Resurrection. Ya' know, if we use our imaginations, we can almost sense Him walking about, his presence everywhere.
We just have to look for Him.

Autumn 2007

Greetings dear friends,

It feels like a long time since last writing to you… now let's see, it must have been around Easter. The summer wasn't too bad, was it? Just a few stretches in the low 90's and high humidity. Thank God for my shed! The horseflies don't usually come in there, so I find some relief from their incessant battering. But my caretakers are really good about spraying me with that sweet-smelling bug repellent. As you know, my only objection is that I smell like a girl. It's really embarrassing.

And once again, the days are already getting shorter, and the nights chilly. I am so lucky to be outside all the time, under the stars - I feel sorry for those poor horses that are cooped up in stalls. I really have the good life…

Why not consider sleeping out here on the grass sometime. You're welcome to find a spot in my enclosure. Plenty of room, actually. You just have to be careful of where you're walking, though. It doesn't bother me - I just walk right through it. After all, I left those piles there.

I wish you all a lovely autumn. Take some time for enjoying the crisp clear air and the gorgeous colors…

I said to my soul,
  Be still,
and let the dark come upon you
which shall be the darkness of God.

  I said to my soul,
    Be still,
  and wait without hope
  for hope would be hope for the wrong thing...

    Wait without love
    for love would be love of the wrong thing;

      There is yet faith...
      But the faith and the love and the hope
      are all in the waiting.

  Wait without thought
  for you are not ready for thought.

So the darkness shall be
    the light,
    and the stillness, the dancing.   *T.S. Eliot "Four Quartets."*

143

Spring 2008

And a glorious salutation to you all on this beautiful day! Not difficult to imagine heaven on a day like this with the clouds softly wafting by, and a slight breeze gently moving the branches. The leaves now are that fresh green, almost iridescent against the backdrop of blue sky.

Hope you had a meaningful Easter. Sorry we couldn't get the newsletter out before this, but at least we can wish you a joy-filled Ascensiontide. For those of you who may not be familiar with some of these terms, the Ascension was when Jesus went up to heaven.

Let's place ourselves back there in Jesus' time. He was dead, and then alive. Around for another 40 days, and now is gone. Imagine how all his followers felt. There must have been a sense of anxiety and fear. No wonder they holed themselves up, hiding out from everyone. When he departed from them, did he want them to be huddled in fear?

If we really catch the spirit of Ascensiontide, all anxiety and worry would be transcended. And what remains?
Peace...

Have a wonderful Spring and Summer, friends... take the time to experience the sound of the wind in the leaves, the rain on the roof, the birds singing. Life is good.

Fall 2008

Greetings to all our friends! What a wonderful summer we've had. Do you ever remember such a lovely month of August? Well, for those of us who live in New Jersey, the weather's been perfect. The days have been seasonally hot, but without that oppressive humidity that is so common in this part of the country. And after the sun goes down, the chorus of crickets begins… only to increase in volume to a veritable cacophony through most of the night.

Oh, just to fill you all in on what's happening in my world out here, back behind the convent. Lots of activity, believe me! Early in the summer some men arrived with trucks. I had no idea what was going on, but before long they were hauling huge pieces out of the basement (I believe it was the old furnace.) At first I liked to watch them, but I figured they knew what they were doing, so I went out back farther to graze (and as you all know by now, grazing is my joy.)

Autumn is in the air. Some leaves are already beginning to turn. The change of the seasons is wonderful, isn't it? Golly, the next time you'll be receiving the newsletter there might be snow on the ground!

Live each day to the fullest. Our lives come 'round just once.

Winter 2008

Is it possible Christmas is approaching once again? It seems only a short while ago that the ground was softening, and little green shoots were springing up through the earth. The seasons come round so quickly, don't they? As you all know, there's a lot of time out here to spend contemplating nature and God's amazing blessings. Autumn was so lovely this year, lingering on longer than usual. And by now, hours of daylight are diminished to almost the shortest in the year.

And we wait... we wait patiently, knowing the darkness won't be much longer.

This season of Advent is so wonderful, yes, full of wonder... there is a gentle mystery surrounding this time of year. It's not difficult for me to be aware of the subtle changes throughout each day, but then, I don't have anything else to do than to just 'be'... to listen, watch, and wait.

May your Christmas be filled with the blessings of love, peace and hope. you feel the wonderment of a child when that Holy Babe is born in our hearts once again.

Spring 2009

And a Joyous Eastertide to you all. We have several chances to catch the Spirit of Christ's Resurrection, not only on that glorious morning. What a beautiful Spring we're having, cool enough so the buds are gradually emerging from their protective shells. It is so wonderful to be able to have the time to experience the changes that seem to be happening in front of my eyes!

Easter morning was like a miracle… a full moon beginning its descent behind the evergreens near St Marguerites, and the slow gentle turning from night to morning as the light gradually changed. The birds sleepily started chirping just about the time the New Fire was lit out on the Cloister.

May your Spring and summer be filled with wonder…

Fall 2009

Ahhhh, Autumn. Don't you love the Fall? Everyone just seems to walk with a bounce in their step, with more energy and enthusiasm. Even the birds and squirrels seem to be scurrying about with a kind of busy-ness that is different than the summer. As far as I am concerned, it is such a relief not to be bothered with so many of those dreaded flies. Believe me, you have no idea what it's like! Of course, as I've said often over the years, it is not easy to have to endure that sweet-smelling Avon Skin So Soft they spray me with. Nevertheless, I should just be grateful they care enough about me. Every morning and afternoon they take the time to be sure I am protected from those little buggers.

Anyway, enjoy the change of seasons. Take the time to go for walks, shuffling through the leaves. Just think what's ahead! The colors changing to russets and golds and crimsons.

I've said it before, and I'll say it again. What a miracle each year… soak it all up.

And be thankful.

Christmas 2009

Oh, greetings to all of you this wonder-filled season! Advent is without a doubt a favorite time of year for many, as well as yours truly. I love to be present when the night is at its darkest, just before dawn. The stars seem so close! Did you know that the ancient constellation Orion is mentioned in Homer's Odyssey? And Euripides makes some reference to the unique picture in the heavens. Recently Orion has been hovering over the western horizon just before any glimpse of daylight in the East. It's almost as if the warrior-hunter slips behind the horizon, taking the night with him... (I know, sometimes I can get rather deep. But you all must remember I spend lots of time out here.)

Don't forget, it is the season once more for reflection. If we can only put aside a few moments to take in the quietude of the long nights. Light a candle, play soft music, listen to the crackling of an open fireplace.

Once again, Christmas is not only about presents...
it's also about "Presence."

Enjoy your winter. Come visit us, we'd love to see you.

Do you know what year this was? It was when I first was
found roaming around the Convent and School properties.
A few of the sisters were out walking and found me back in
the woods. Quite frankly, I was a little groggy when this
photo was taken because it was just after I was hit with a
tranquilizer darts a few times (of course the sisters had no
idea all this was going on).

The days are growing longer, lasting well into the evening.
Ah, Spring, oh Spring… so hard to imagine or remember
when in the midst of a winter like the one we just had. As
you know, the first signs are always the snowdrops, which
grow in abundance back here where I hang out. And the
birds are just a cacophony of sounds, especially early in the
morning. The warmth of the sun is almost too much to take
after the winter storms we've had. If you come outside, and
are very still, you can just about hear the sap running
through the trees, and the flowers slowly working their way
up through the dark earth… resurrection.

Hope you have a wonderful Easter and Spring, filled with
blessings and new life.   *(p.s. the photo is from 1992)*

Fall 2010

Oh, hello everyone… hope your summer was as lovely as mine. The heat doesn't seem to bother me, so I am out grazing even mid-day. Quite frankly, the flies don't seem to like the sun, so that is one advantage for the hot summer days (although as I've said before, those dreadful horse flies are the bane of my existence… thank God I can go into my shed to get away from them.)

It's getting darker earlier and earlier, quietly enveloping us in the coolness after the sun sets. I love this time of the evening, don't you? I think the sisters have a phrase, "the Vesper Light." I can hear their voices singing when they have the chapel windows open.
I just stand very still by the fence, listening to the birds, the sound of the rustling leaves, and the sisters' voices all blending together…

Well, as autumn returns once again, I hope the days ahead are full with joy-filled moments for you. Remember to take the time to walk through the dried leaves, taking in the magnificent colors and the delicious air…
and give thanks.

Winter 2010

Ah, yes… and here we are again in the season following Christmas called Epiphanytide. There is nothing like a winter's day with snow on the ground, a vibrant blue sky, and the sun so pure and sparkling. I love a day like that, don't you? Even the trees take on a different appearance in the winter, like sentinels guarding the earth. Yet there is something very vulnerable about trees without their leaves, isn't there? Open and exposed to the elements of wind and ice, they withstand quite a battering. Yet the hope of Spring brings new life every year, and re-birth…

These winter nights are so clear, and still. The first light of dawn often seems to take so long to arrive, yet when it does, it is worth the wait… the birds begin their chirping, soon to be fluttering all around the feeders.

I wish for you a winter filled with blessings, and a time of reflective creativity. Try taking up something new like knitting or needlepoint. And perhaps find a moment here and there to pause and linger, in wonderment and awe of God's presence.

Spring 2011

Easter Blessings this wonderful spring day. The signs of new life and resurrection can be seen everywhere - new shoots pushing up through the earth, snowdrops, crocuses, daffodils… it's hard to imagine that only a month ago the ground was still hard underhoof, with snow and ice that just wouldn't melt. Spring seemed to take forever this year, didn't it?

By now I am sure you heard the sad news about Petie. He crossed over the Rainbow Bridge just recently. We think he had a stroke at the end because he couldn't stand up.

Oh, we had great times when we both were a lot younger. We were such good friends.

I will truly miss you…

Autumn 2011
Hello, everyone… I hope you had a good summer.
I certainly did.

There's been a lot going on here at the convent! It seemed
men were climbing all over the building, and quite frankly
I didn't know what they were doing. As the days wore on,
there was hammering and clanking of metal. And now in
the back and the side of the building there is a metal
structure, with stairs going up and walkways. They started
taking out some windows last week! At first it was upsetting,
because I didn't know what they were doing to my beloved
convent. But the sisters didn't seem to be concerned, so I
just went back to eating.

Well, the days are getting shorter so we know the summer is
comimg to a close. I really don't mind… as you know, I love
the autumn.

I hope you have a wonderful fall.

There's so much to be thankful for, isn't there?

Winter 2011

As you all know already, Advent and Christmastide are two of my favorite seasons in the year. There is something so holy about the stillness of a cold winter's night, when you can almost hear soft music in the air... or is it the sound of angels' wings?

Winter lends itself to letting go, giving us the opportunity to shed whatever it is that encumbers us from the things that really matter. What *really* is important to you? What are the things in your own life that you could not be without?
Ah, it may have occurred to you this might not be very characteristic of me to be so philosophical. After all, I'm only a small horse that lives outside, leading a simple and uncomplicated life. But I have a lot of time to think, and ponder...

Take a moment here and there, and pause... and perhaps you also will hear the sound of angels' wings.

Spring 2012

Well, if any of you have been to the convent lately, you will see all the construction still happening. I don't know how the sisters can take all the noise… and the jackhammer on the front cloister! Oh my.

Ah, but the workers leave when the sun goes down, and quiet once again pervades the grounds, and I can resume my grazing in peace.

The birds are chirping, and the tree toads (peepers) have begun their Spring chorus. The nights are still, the stars brighter than ever. It's hard to believe it's Spring.

I certainly hope your Easter is filled with blessings.

Cherish, hold closely the New Life all around you.

Fall 2012

Greetings to all on this glorious bright and shiny day! The sky is that vibrant blue, with small puffy white clouds slowly meandering by. The birds are hustling about, and the hummingbirds are swirling around their feeders. Soon they will be gone and on their long journey to South America... truly amazing.

When autumn arrives, there is something almost electrifying in the air. Hopefully, you all can put aside some time in your week to enjoy the Fall.
We only get to do this earthly life one time around.
Think about that...

Advent 2012

Oh, hello everyone… so good to connect with you all again. It's that time of year once more, when the days are getting shorter and shorter, and the nights longer. It takes some getting used to, doesn't it? I know that some of my friends (two legged and four) don't like it when it gets darker so much earlier. Yet, if we look at it as an opportunity to slow down and perhaps be more reflective it might change the way we look at the whole thing.

Living outside like I do, there are no distractions like TVs or computers or iPhones. It's really quite lovely, standing motionless under the stars on a still, cold winter's night, or when a snowfall starts. Have you ever been outside when the snow begins to fall? If you really listen closely, you can hear it when it touches the earth.

Then in the morning being warmed from the sun…
Don't know about you, but I really long for more of those moments.

May you find peace, love and joy this wonder-filled season. Hopefully, you can spend some time with friends or family.

Spring 2013

Spring is here at last, and the blossoming fruit trees are just blooming out of control. Of course, the grass is coming up back here (finally), so I am in heaven grazing to my heart's content. I am getting to be an old guy, so my teeth are not the greatest anymore. But the sisters are sensitive to my limitations, so they changed my diet to Equine Senior pellets that they water down. Of course, grass is very easy to chew, so as I said, I am happy.

The winter was not as bad as some, although there were a few very cold patches. Every night one of the sisters (it is usually Sr Margo) would come out with a warm gruel that was just right, warming up my insides, getting me through until dawn.

(Spring 2013 continued...)

So much going on here during this past month, and I'm not quite sure what it was all about! There were lots of people, led by bagpipes and banners. I was getting a little nervous as I thought they were coming back into my area. But they stopped at the corner of the convent building and just said a few prayers.

What really was a little strange was something smoking on the end of a chain, and someone was swinging it from side to side... I don't know, these humans have some funny habits!

I certainly hope you all enjoy the remainder of spring.

Fall 2013

It's once again time for a newsletter! I get the feeling you all have heard so much of this before. I don't want to bore you with repetition. Yet, living out here in the back enclosure can be, well, rather routine. You know, just hanging out, day after day. But, on the other hand, one can learn a lot from living simply. I have everything I need, really... shelter from the wind and rain; plenty of grass, fresh water and hay; protection from the flies (they spray me twice a day in the hot weather). Back to basics, I always say...

So, when all my needs are met, I can spend more time contemplating God's creation!

I love watching for the sunrise. I try to stand in just the right spot for that breaking of a new day. Oh, and listening for the first bird each morning. Sometimes it's a Robin, or maybe a Carolina Wren... and of course, later in the morning, or just around sunset from May through July, one can almost be transported by the sound of the Thrush. I just love the Thrush's song, don't you?

Have a great autumn. Live each moment to the fullest.

Winter 2013

Greetings, dear friends. I just can't imagine living in any other part of the country where there aren't four distinct seasons to mark the year. In autumn, as oftentimes said before, I just love to walk through my back enclosure through the fallen leaves, breathing in the cool, clean autumn air. The grass isn't great anymore, yet the leaves are rather a delicacy (it's called foraging, which a creature like myself does rather well.)

Winter has arrived, but my shed is insulated now (well, the top of it, anyway) so the nights won't be so cold. My coat is thick and toasty, so I stay quite warm, even in the freezing rain and snow.

Please notice the Christmas wreath on my shed. It really gets me into the spirit of the season. The sisters remember to put one up every year (but sometimes forget to take it down, often still there until Easter!) But I don't mind...

Prayers for the upcoming Advent and Christmas seasons, a time to slow down and ponder the wonders of Creation... listen to a gentle snowfall, perhaps feed the birds, go out on a cold night and look up at the stars... and be grateful.

Easter 2014

Don't know about you all, but I thought this past winter was brutal. I can't remember a winter where the nights dipped down into the teens so often, with snowfall after snowfall. And the ice on top of that! The sisters always worry about me, that I might slip on the ice. But I am very careful, walking very slowly and deliberately, trying to avoid the icy patches. They often throw something down on the ice so it won't be so dangerous (they do watch out for me...)

Well, spring is in the air, I promise you... the birds are singing, the snowdrops are coming up, and the days are growing longer. The hope of warmer weather is around the corner. Just wait, we all will be complaining about the heat before long! And then I have to deal with the flies... and of course they spray me with that sweet-smelling Avon Skin So Soft that I really hated in the beginning, but it is effective. Why not try it. It really works...

May your Easter be filled with the Blessings of hope and New Life.

Celebrate being alive...

Fall 2014

Well, the summer wasn't too bad, was it? I guess by now those of us who live here are accustomed to the typical New Jersey humidity. It really doesn't get to me that much, thank God, even if I don't have the luxury of air conditioning. As you know, there are lots of shady spots back here. And of course, there is my shed. Quite frankly, I don't think I'd like AC. I rather be out in nature spending time with all God's Creation.

Once again, the time of year is here when the days and nights grow cooler and the leaves fall from the trees. It is such an honor to be able to be here and experience the rhythm of the seasons, year after year. My life is quite simple really, as you already know. Each year I am blessed to witness nature's gentle cycle as it unfolds… so very uncomplicated.

I hope you all have the opportunity to experience the subtle changes each day.
Life is precious.

Carpe diem.

Christmas 2014

Ah, and here we are again, full circle, to Advent and Christmastide (and to be sure, by the time this gets to you, it may be after Christmas!) If we are lucky, the coming Winter might be more forgiving than last year. So far it really hasn't been too bad, has it? As long as there is no snow on the ground, there is still always some grass to munch on, and anything else that might be back here in my larger enclosure (remember, I am one of those foraging beasts!) The sisters are good to me, softening the Timothy pellets they now give me. The apples have to be cored and the carrots grated (some of my teeth are not there anymore.)

Did you all know I've been here for over 23 years, and they think I was already 7 or 8 years old when I arrived. Hey, that makes me close to 30 years old! It's been a good life, living back here on the convent grounds. Nothing to complain about…

Blessings to you all during this very Holy Season. Perhaps spend some time outside after a snowfall… does the soul good.

Spring 2015

Greetings all! Well, we thought the previous winter was brutal, yet the one we just managed to get through was equally as bad. I think the snow was covering the ground from around the third week of January to the middle of March. It seemed to take forever for the flowers to begin to come up from the hard earth. And although Spring has begun to bloom, the warmth of the season is taking its sweet time! Yesterday we had a few white particles drifting down from the sky (I chose to continue grazing and managed to ignore that...) Yet, they say the things we have to wait for we cherish more. Hm. At least it will be a slow gradual emerging of new life rather than going quickly from winter to summer.

Well, regardless of how many Springs I've experienced, every year I just am in awe. Especially when all still appears to be dead from the grips of winter, here and there emerges some green shoots, the first signs of new life... ah, if that's not Resurrection I don't know what is!

Enjoy each new day.

Celebrate life.

Fall 2015

And a warm hello to all our friends on this lovely September day! We hope that you enjoyed your summer and had a chance to get away to a favorite place. Did your vacations seem to end too quickly? We always know when summer is coming to a close when we can hear the sound of the katydids at night, in the beginning of August.

I really look forward to the autumn, the changing colors of the trees, those crisp mornings when you can see the vapor of your breath, shuffling through the dried leaves… and the sky almost an iridescent blue. Ah, it's good to be alive on those days. And the night skies! Oh, the night skies, when you can almost reach up and touch the stars…

I heard that the Pope came to visit us recently here in the states. So many people like Pope Francis, and we don't have to be a Catholic to really appreciate him. He doesn't put on any airs. No pretenses about him.
I wonder if he likes horses…

Have a wonder-filled autumn. Pick up some apple cider and think of me.

Winter 2015
A Blessed Advent, Christmastide and Epiphany to you, whatever the case may be (depending on when the newsletter goes out!)

So, how was your autumn? Well, here the weather so far has been rather forgiving, with mild days, and nights that are not too cold. I don't think we've had a deep freeze yet, so there's still lots of grass out back to spend hours of grazing, which as you know is heaven for me. But I'm ready for the change in the weather. I've grown my whiskers and thick coat that will get me through the cold winter nights.

I know it is crazy busy time of year, with all your Christmas shopping. But if you could allow a few minutes a day for some quiet. And let's not forget all those who are alone or who need our prayers…
Count your blessings.

Spring 2016
May the Blessings of Spring/Summer be with each of you!
The winter wasn't too bad, was it. Actually, it was rather
forgiving, don't you think?

Each season has some sort of challenge, for an outdoors guy
like myself. If it's not the ice in winter, it's those little gnats
in Spring and the dreaded horse flies in Summer. I actually
spend more time in my shed in the summer months than the
colder ones. And the scent of the fresh pine bedding smells
so good! I am well cared for, by the sisters as well as Ken
and his son Ryan.

(...this is Ryan, one of my favorite humans)

Ryan often scrubs my water basin, so I always have fresh,
clean water to drink. And of course, all my woodland friends
help themselves - the birds, squirrels, chipmunks, deer, and
foxes (and the dog and cat.)

As long as I have plenty to eat, fresh water, protection from
the flies, and a shed for warmth in the winter, I have no
complaints.

God is good. All the time...

Autumn 2016

Greetings, dear friends… Well, I hope your summer was refreshing and you had a restful, fun vacation. The seasonal weather seemed to last right up until recently, when we had a few very warm days. But alas, the leaves are falling, and the nights are getting cooler. My winter coat is already thick, so I am feeling quite comfortable (except on those hot days!)

Oh, before I forget, if you happen to stop by for a visit, you'll notice I have a new post and rail fence. The work was done by a young man named Brian Schultz who was working to move up to Eagle Scout level. We want to thank him for all his hard work.

Hope you have a wonderful autumn…

(an early dusting of snow and my new fencing…)

December 2016
I can't tell you enough how lucky I am to be living out here!
Every once in a while, I can get a quick take on the news,
and believe me, these last few months were unforgettable.
They elected a new president of the United States!
Sometimes the radio on the truck is quite loud when they are
pulling up to the carport, or on one of the cars when pulling
into the garages. The newscasters' voices sounded so
excited, talking so fast I didn't always catch what the words
were.

And in contrast, it is so peaceful back here...

May your Christmas season and the next year be one that is
filled with many blessings.

It was a lovely morning one day in the early Spring. There was a small opening in my fence that was just too tempting to ignore. I decided to go for a stroll down our road. I was gone for about 36 hours they tell me. Had a great time, but really began to get confused. The big white building that they call the school looked a lot like the convent, and soon I realized I had wandered farther than I thought. Trotting down the hill behind the school, toward the pond in the back, I found the old hockey field. I spent the whole night there. But alas, the following day it was time for my late afternoon meal, and Ryan approached with my feed (I think Sr Margo had something to do with it and added some molasses to it.) It smelled awful good! So, I followed Ryan, past the pond, through the woods and up the hill along the convent wall. We made it to the side of the building, opposite the main chapel, and I found some nice grass. It must have been the time for Ryan's day to be over, so he left. Before long the sun was setting, and Sr Margo appeared. She sat down on the bench near the Oregon Pine with that delicious smelling container of feed in her hands. I decided to throw in the towel and followed her back to my enclosure.
It was a great night out on the town!

Fall 2017

Greetings, everyone! Well, when this was written, the weather had been absolutely glorious. The month of October is so special, especially the quality of light… "the golden days of October." So true…

Please forgive me. I am aware that there are some things I always seem to talk about. Light is so important to me. To be honest, it is the one source where I always find God.

The days are getting cooler and before long those wonderful crisp autumn days will be here again.

Maybe you can go out and get some apple cider, or pick up a pumpkin or two, and perhaps a mum plant!
Carpe Diem.

Christmas 2017
We had our first snowfall of the season. It didn't amount to much, only an inch or two. And then the sun came out. It was warm and it felt so good.

I just stood there, soaking up the warmth, and the silence. It was so lovely.

Silence is something a lot of people feel uncomfortable with. I think you know already, if I were to say when I feel God's Presence more than any other time, it's in silence, in stillness…

Have a wonderful Christmas and a healthy New Year. And let's hope the winter isn't too bad.

Spring 2018

Hi everyone,

Greetings on this lovely spring day! Oh, but let's catch up…
In March we had a bad storm, and as you can see, we had
quite a lot of uprooted trees on our property. But thanks to
Pat Donnelly my area was cleared away. I was very lucky
because a huge tree fell within feet of my shed.
Thank God I was not injured.
And hopefully you are all OK.

Eastertide Blessings to everyone! And I would like to say,
Happy Spring. But alas, when writing this, it still feels like
winter!

There are a few signs of new life, to be sure… green shoots
springing from the earth, and the yellow forsythia bushes
beginning to burst forth into singing! The snowdrops were
the first to appear, as they do every year. Ah, the harbingers
of spring they are...
Enjoy the weeks ahead.

Take time to pause and be witness to new life everywhere.

Fall 2018

At last, Autumn weather is finally here. Isn't it wonderful?
The nights are crisp, the air clean and fresh. Some say we
won't get a spectacular display of colors. With all the rain
we've had! But you know what? We just cannot control
everything, can we? When will we ever learn to just put our
trust in God? Obviously, I'm not just talking about the fall
colors, or the weather… we need to get out of the way and
place ourselves in God's care. It's that simple. Yet very
difficult. We want to be in control.

Have you ever seen the bumper stickers, "LET GO, LET
GOD" and "BELIEVE IN MIRACLES…" (you're probably
wondering how I'd seen bumper stickers? Don't forget,
numerous cars and trucks come to our back parking lot!)

Believe in miracles. I do.

Winter 2018

And a warm hello to you all! I hope you had a good Christmas and are surviving the cold weather. From my perspective, so far it hasn't been too difficult a season, well, so far anyway. Not too much snow, yet we are getting those Polar Vortex events again. The week I am writing this we are supposed to be having a few days in the single digits. But I am not too concerned as I have a thick winter coat that keeps me quite warm, and am really enjoying spending more time in my shed, curling up in the corner in the fluffy pine shavings. And 3 times a day I get a warm mash, which I really look forward to eating. When I see someone coming out with it, as they approach, I try to help by pushing my "bowl" under the fence toward them. They seem to appreciate that...

Oh, there was a whole flock of robins on the cedar trees in my back enclosure. A wonderful sign of Spring, filled with hope and the promise of new life...

Spring 2019
It's so good to be in touch with you all again. Doesn't it seem ages since we connected? Those cold winter months are behind us now, thank God.

Spring is indeed coming, although I do appear somewhat dubious in this photo, don't I.

We can look forward to a glorious Easter morning, when the chains of death are shattered, and the world is filled with Light.

Eastertide is with us for weeks, and every day there are new signs of life. Each year I am so aware of the miracle of spring, as you all already know. Resurrection can be seen and felt everywhere. I can almost hear God's voice resounding loud and clear, "Behold, I make all things new!"

Take the time to watch clouds, listen to the rain, smell the flowers...

Fall 2019

Dear ones. I am sure this will come as a shock, but some of you don't know that left this earthly home and crossed over the Rainbow Bridge in June. It was very peaceful. Please don't be sad. I had a great life and am so very grateful to the sisters and others who cared for me for all those years.

I would like to share a favorite poem.

"Do not stand at my grave and weep
I am not there; I do not sleep.
I am a thousand winds that blow,
I am the diamond glints on snow,
I am the sun on ripened grain,
I am the gentle autumn rain.
When you awaken in the morning's hush
I am the swift uplifting rush
Of quiet birds in circled flight.
I am the soft stars that shine at night.
Do not stand at my grave and cry,
I am not there; I did not die..."

Mary Elizabeth Frye

About the Author

M.E. Colman is a life-professed member of the Convent of St. John Baptist, an Episcopal religious community for women in Mendham, N.J. Before becoming a nun, Sister Margo had a varied background in music, art, and psychology, completing her undergraduate work in Fine Arts and Psychology and graduate work in Human Development, receiving both degrees from Farleigh Dickinson University. During these years Margo worked as an artist for an engraving firm, taught individual flute lessons, performed with a harpsichordist playing Baroque music, and was a teacher-therapist for emotionally disturbed children.

Once entering the religious life, for many years Sister Margo was in charge of the community's retreat and conference center, St. Marguerite's. She is an experienced spiritual director with training in Ignatian Spirituality. Her varied background in the arts and psychology often come into play when guiding others.

Since 1999, Sr. Margo has led groups to Ireland, Scotland, Wales and Cornwall. Upon returning from one of her Ireland trips, she felt moved to write a book about the people in Ireland. "Sometimes a Star" encompasses candid conversations with 20 individuals in Ireland. They are asked questions such as, "what sustains you" and "where do you find God," leading inevitably to dialogue that is rich with honesty and humor.

Currently Sr. Margo continues to do spiritual direction and leads groups to Ireland and the UK. After finishing the present book, she hopes to republish *Sometimes a Star*.

Sr. Margo is passionate about wildlife preservation and the environment. Her love of nature and animals clearly is evident in her writing.